A Welsh Saint

THE KEL COSLETT STORY

A Welsh Saint

THE KEL COSLETT STORY

Kel Coslett with Mike Appleton

VERTICAL EDITIONS

www.verticaleditions.com

First published in the United Kingdom in 2010 by Vertical Editions, Unit 4a, Snaygill Industrial Estate, Skipton, North Yorkshire BD23 2QR

www.verticaleditions.com

A CIP catalogue record for this book is available from the British Library

ISBN 978-1-904091-35-6

Cover design and typeset by HBA, York

Printed and bound by The MPG Books Group, Bodmin

CONTENTS

Dedicated to Jacqueline, my wonderful daughters and fantastic grandchildren. Without you I wouldn't be where I am today.

ACKNOWLEDGEMENTS

We couldn't possibly name everyone who has been involved in the writing of this book, or even begin to mention those of you who have helped Kel Coslett throughout his career. You know who you are and therefore we apologise for any omissions here.

Firstly, we'd like to thank the players, supporters and staff at St Helens RLFC over the past 40 or so years for making this story happen.

We'd also like to thank Les Williams the Historian at Llanelli RFU, Andrew John and all at Aberavon RU, Dai Morgan, Howard Evans, Peter Richards for his invaluable 1960–61 Aberavon Scrapbook, Geoff Pimblett, Alex Service who proved a rock during the scribing of this tome, Karl Waddicor at Vertical Editions for making it happen, Tony and all the staff at the Black Bull in St Helens for their hospitality and NOT the music, Bill Bates and Ray Fletcher for the statistical support, Mike Critchley from the *St Helens Star*, Nigel McFarlane, Gareth Wright for his picture editing skills, the late Cliff Rance for his superb scrapbooks and everyone who contributed to the tributes' section.

Kel would like to thank his family for all the support they have given him over the years and especially his wife Jacqueline, who has proved a tower of strength throughout the whole writing process.

Mike would like to thank Jacqueline for letting Kel spend

most of his lunchtimes in the Black Bull when he should probably have been 'doing a bit' at home. Mike would also like to thank his own family and friends both for letting him lock himself away as the deadline got closer and for giving him the inspiration to approach Kel in the first place.

Yn ôl ym 1962, pan fyddai rhywun yn mynd 'lan y North' i chwarae rygbi'r gynghrair, roedd y drws yn cau'n glep ar eich ôl—doedd dim gobaith chwarae rygbi'r undeb byth wedyn. Yr argraff oedd na fyddai croeso yn ôl yng Nghymru, ond nid oedd hynny'n wir o gwbl, ac yn sicr nid felly y bu pethau yn fy mhrofiad i. Mae fy nghyd-Gymry wedi fy nghroesawu yn ôl bob amser ac wedi dangos diddordeb yn fy ngyrfa yn Rygbi'r Gynghrair. Roedden nhw'n mwynhau fy llwyddiant gyda mi ac mae gennyf ffrindiau hyd heddiw sy'n fy ffonio ar ôl gemau'r 'Saints'. Hoffwn ddiolch i bawb yng Nghymru sydd wedi fy nghefnogi a'm hannog drwy gydol fy 47 mlynedd yn Rygbi'r Gynghrair. Rwyf wastad wedi gwerthfawrogi hynny'n fawr ac yn parhau i wneud hynny. Mae'r aduniadau yn y Bynea, Llanelli ac Aberafan wedi bod yn bleser pur—dyma uchafbwyntiau'r flwyddyn i mi. Rwyf yn dal i fod wrth fy modd yn gwylio Cymru'n chwarae a theithio i Stadiwm y Mileniwm i gefnogi'r bechgyn—mae'n hyfryd cael dod yn ôl i fy ngwreiddiau. Diolch i'r holl bobl arbennig sydd wedi dangos cymaint o garedigrwydd tuag ataf dros y blynyddoedd.

Back in 1962 when someone 'signed North' there was no going back—you could never again play rugby union. The impression was that you became an outcast in Wales, but nothing could be further from the truth, and this certainly wasn't something I ever experienced. The people from my homeland have always welcomed me back and have shown an interest in my career in rugby league. They enjoyed my success along with me, and I still have friends who call after a Saints match now. I would like to thank everyone in Wales who has supported and encouraged me throughout my 48 years in rugby league; I have always appreciated it so much and still do. I have loved the reunions I have attended in Bynea, Llanelli and Aberavon; they are the highlight of my year. I still love to watch Wales play their internationals and travel to the Millennium Stadium to support them; it's lovely to go back to my roots. Thanks to all the lovely people who have been so kind to me over the years.

I would like to take this opportunity to thank the people of the rugby league world, and the St Helens club and fans in particular, for the help and support I have received since moving to St Helens in 1962. It was difficult to leave home at 20, no one had telephones to keep in touch, and it was like going to the other side of the world. I needn't have worried, you were all so great from the beginning and have remained great for the past 48 years. I couldn't have moved to a better place than St Helens, the people have been warm and generous and I wouldn't have achieved what I have in rugby without their interest and help.

Thank you all.

Kel Coslett
January 2010

In an area where rugby league is king, I was brought up with tales of 'Voll', 'Murph' and co. setting the town alight with their dazzling skills and winning trophy after trophy in the sixties and seventies. But whilst others talked about that amazing winger from South Africa, my old fella said to me, 'Forget all those, Kel was king up there' [jabbing upwards to signal Knowsley Road].

It was only when I started working for the club—after being a 'home and away' fan for many years—that I truly realised what a hero the chap from Bynea in South Wales was. And his stories are legendary.

Throughout the course of this book, I had a great time as Kel recounted tales from his past. Sometimes it was pretty surreal, like when he asked me if I had ever put my finger in a ferret's mouth and other times it was like being out with an old friend.

Most of the time, the Black Bull in St Helens provided a focal point for the anecdotes to flow, alongside a few beers, and several afternoons were lost listening to the dodgiest of eighties' sounds on landlord Tony's jukebox.

Then there were the afternoons spent 'investing' in horses and getting no return whatsoever using Kel's very technical betting formula [his scrawl deciphered from the back of a piece of kitchen roll].

Thanks to everyone who helped along the way (you know who you are). I hope you enjoy reading it as much as Kel and I enjoyed working on it.

Mike Appleton
January 2010

FOREWORD

During my playing days with the St Helens Club, such were the number of former rugby union stars who switched codes and trekked north from the valleys to Knowsley Road, it was a distinct advantage to learn Welsh if you wanted to know what was happening around the scrum.

With John Warlow, John Mantle, Mervyn Hicks and Kel Coslett all packing down around me, and with former Newport scrum half Bob Prosser occasionally putting the ball in the scrum, my own local St Helens' dialect and Cliff Watson's broad Midlands' accent hardly registered.

But all were part of a fine tradition at St Helens, stretching back well over 100 years, a tradition of attracting some of the finest rugby union talent in Wales and converting that talent into equally gifted rugby league players. And no better signing was ever made by the Saints' scouting team than that of Aberavon's fullback, Kel Coslett. Yes, fullback, even though Kel's greatest contribution to St Helens' success in the sixties and the seventies was as a forward.

The statistical records which adorn every rugby league website, every club programme and every yearbook or annual, highlight those players who have made an outstanding contribution to club and country. So it is with Kel, but his amazing scoring feats only serve to show just one aspect of the incredible service he has made to the St Helens Club both on and off the pitch.

His playing and points scoring record fully indicates just what his presence meant to his teammates around him. Between 1962 and 1976 he played a record 531 games for his club and scored a staggering club record 3,413 points. That took some scoring, but then he was some player. Statistics do not tell the full contribution to a club, nor do they tell much of the man and his impact on his teammates.

That Kel had the determination to succeed in his new code is easily seen, when, in only his third season at Knowsley Road, he fractured his leg and suffered so many other injuries that his appearances were severely restricted for the next two years. He finally reappeared in the famous red and white jersey as a loose forward and later as a prop. And so began a great career as a leader and a captain both on and off the field.

As a teammate, Kel had the passion, the spirit and the love of the game which often helped to raise the efforts of those of us playing alongside him. As a captain, he not only had the tactical knowledge and leadership which instils confidence in others but always had the compassion and concern for those players perhaps not as gifted as himself.

Such qualities have also proved to be of immense value to all around him at Knowsley Road during his continued service and loyalty to the club (shown in many guises) for the past 30 years at least. Today, Kel Coslett will be regarded as Saints' most prolific point scorer, as a superbly adaptable player whatever his position and as one of his club's finest ever captains.

To those, like me, who had the honour of playing alongside him and of working with him in recent years in his many capacities off the pitch at Knowsley Road, he will always be a true friend, one for whom you would always 'go the extra mile', and a player who ever commanded your respect.

He was a gentleman who could play rugby league (and union) like few others and whose continued loyalty and service to St Helens serves as an example to others. I am sure such qualities, as well as the fascinating details of his lengthy career, will prove to be a central feature of his story in this book.

Ray French, *January 2010*

1

'ALL I EVER WANTED TO DO WAS PLAY…'

Rugby league is much like the community I came from. Like Bynea in South Wales, rugby people are close knit, know each other's business and most of the time get on. That's not to say there isn't the odd spat now and again, but as time goes by it becomes part of your life…part of you.

I've been involved in the sport for nearly half a century and it has given me the best and worst of times. I have experienced the highs and lows. But, above all, it has given me a sense of being. At the start of the sixties no one knew that the decade was set to change the culture of the country; similarly, at the start of the sixties, little did I know that my decision to head north would lead to so many friends and fond memories.

When I decided to sign on for St Helens Rugby League Club, I didn't know exactly why I made the move. Suffice to say; I never really understood the magnitude of the decision until I broke my leg a few seasons later. People can get misty eyed about why players move to certain clubs, but I'm going to be straight from the start. When I signed on the dotted line, it was firstly for financial gain and secondly, but still importantly, for the challenge.

Lionel Swift and Basil Lowe sat in my house, drinking my

mother's whisky and the offer they put on the table was too good to turn down. I scribbled 'Thomas Kelvin Coslett' on the dotted line and I can honestly say I have never regretted that decision. The people I have met along the way, the players, fans and officials have made me what I am. They are part of me and will stick with me forever.

Before I signed, I played rugby union in an area of Wales where the game is like a religion. The team I played for were total amateurs and who can blame a 20-year-old kid for taking the money and coming north? I didn't realise the challenges that lay ahead of me and still, to this day, the challenges come thick and fast.

I missed out on the Lions tour to South Africa because a player who was basically playing for fun over there was picked ahead of me. A player had been injured and he was on hand to come in. That was a disappointment and perhaps I can use it as an excuse for joining Saints. Or one of the reasons anyway. You could say I was a bit young to be disappointed, because I was lucky enough to be in a position to be considered, but the disappointment of not being sent for was massive. All I ever wanted to do was play.

I played rugby union for my school, village and town team and I was lucky enough to be spotted, picked up and subsequently chosen to play in so many great teams. I trained with the likes of Welsh international Terry Davies who came from the same village as me and his sheer enthusiasm for me to succeed drove me forward. I trained with Llanelli, although I couldn't play for them until I was 18. I was lucky that when I turned 18 I became eligible for Llanelli as that is where my rugby career took off. I couldn't have planned it better and it's lovely really.

This shows how good people have been to me. This includes the likes of Terry, my teachers and the people with Llanelli schoolboys. Coincidentally, some teachers left the committee of

Llanelli schoolboys and went on to the committee of Llanelli first team. This meant that when I became 18 and eligible for the first team, there were people on the committee that I was friendly with. What I'm saying is you have to be lucky to get to where you are; you must keep plugging away to reach your goals. Even now the people who put me on the road to Saints, where I made so many friendships, are still close to me.

Whether or not people thought at the time I was making the right choice is debatable, but talking about it today, I think that most people would say it was the right thing to do, because I'm still part of the game, and I've enjoyed playing it over the years. Although I am now Life President of the club I first played with in rugby league, I still don't, and never did, consider myself that special. I just consider myself very lucky indeed. I was lucky to have the opportunity to score points wherever I went and to set a record point's haul at Saints that probably won't be beaten.

As a kid I always kicked goals. When I played for Llanelli schoolboys I was the biggest kid in the team. Size meant responsibility and that meant kicking. Terry Davies saw this and told my dad, 'Tell Kel I'm taking him down to Llanelli at six o'clock to train with us.' I just went and trained with them. These days I'm still taking orders mostly from the wife I first met in St Helens but also from the players.

I know it's a cliché, but I can't believe I have been in St Helens for so long. It doesn't seem like yesterday I caught the train with the locals from Bynea presenting me with an electric razor and waving me off. When I arrived at Lime Street in Liverpool, Stan McCormack—Saints coach—and Secretary Basil Lowe met me and Stan said: 'You want to enjoy this, it will soon be over. If you do 10 years you'll be lucky.'

The sport has given me so many close friends and friends of friends that when I go out I often get recognised. It does have its downsides though. When I left Saints in 1982, after a decent spell as coach, I quickly disappeared from view. I was out of the game at a time when I thought I should not have been. My wife was delighted because she saw a difference in people's attitude to a coach's wife, as compared to their attitude to a player's wife. But I accepted it and tried to get on.

Then I was lucky that Silk Cut sponsored the Challenge Cup through Gallagher and they wanted some ex-rugby league players to take them to the game. In the nineties I became involved in the marketing side of Saints and then became Football Manager when Eric Hughes left.

Sport has a nasty habit of kicking people out. One day you are up, then suddenly you are fired and the game moves on. It can make you fall out of love with the sport, but this element will always be there. I know you are only as good as your last performance and all that, but things aren't always done right in rugby.

Lots of players will have a sob story and say they have been unfairly done to. But you have to take the good with the bad—lots of things could have been done more fairly. Lots of players have been stopped from playing the game without the reasons behind it being explained to them.

I was lucky because after leaving, I returned to the game fairly quickly to work behind the scenes. But then, I always worked for the chances and they came good for me. With my kicking, I used to practise a lot. I would always be last in—and it would get lonely. There was many a time I would be out there kicking and thinking, 'What the bloody hell am I doing out here?' It was always about preparation for me and I still do that to this day. I am meticulous with everything I do and it's a mantra that stands me in good stead.

My story is a simple one…it's down to luck and taking the chances that are presented. You have to work hard when chances come your way, as they may never come around again.

2

'I NEVER THOUGHT OF THE FUTURE AT ALL WHEN I WAS A KID...'

I grew up in a small village called Pen-y-graig just outside Bynea, which literally means 'on top of the hill' in Welsh. It was half a mile from the main road from Llanelli to Swansea and I lived in a cul-de-sac at the edge of a large council estate.

There were plenty of fields around where the village kids got together and threw a rugby ball about, kicked a football or played cricket. Some would say it was idyllic—you could see the sea from the top bedroom of my house and there was very little traffic. Kids in the village walked to school and caught a bus to Llanelli (once old enough to go secondary school). But we rarely went out of the area unless we were going on holiday, which wasn't too often. 'Town' (or Llanelli) was literally the furthest we went—we only went there for school or to go to the pictures. And we only did this when we were deemed to be old enough.

Sport was the staple diet of the kids in the area. We played football, cricket or rugby and that was it. As well as having friends in the area, I had loads of cousins living close by so never really struggled to find someone to play with. The cul-de-sac I lived in had 24 houses and two of my aunties lived opposite.

People in the village worked in Port Talbot for the Steel Company of Wales, put in the hours at Buckley's Brewery or worked down the mines. Two of my cousins were killed in a mine explosion at Llangennech—one, Graham, was only 18 at the time. Graham Coslett was a fine rugby player and had already played for Wales at youth level, so the explosion snuffed out a potentially great rugby career. After this, as I grew older, my mother didn't want me to work in the pits even though most of my relatives worked there. Thankfully, to this day, I have never been underground. We didn't think about those kinds of things back then as we were only young and people needed to make a living. The dangers of mining were an occupational hazard.

Rugby was a big thing in the area and the successful career of Terry Davies proved that lads from the valleys could, with hard work and dedication, make it big. I never thought about making it as a player though. Even from a young age I just wanted to play and nothing else really mattered as long as I had a ball in my hand and someone else wanted to play with me.

Growing up was a great time for me. Because my cousins lived so close by, we were all one big, happy family. I was close to both my mum and dad and my only brother, Keri. Although there are 12 years between Keri and I, we were, and still are, very close. When he was born I used to babysit and push him around. Like me, he played rugby. He captained Welsh youth and also turned out for Llanelli and Aberavon as a centre/stand off and did all right. Now, he's a financial advisor—he's making the money and I'm spending it!

Perhaps it was a bit unfair for him growing up as my brother and I suppose living in my shadow. But he grew up with my friends and whenever I was about, so was he. Whether Keri was always known as 'Kelvin's brother' I don't know. It might have been a little disheartening for him at times. But, we were all one big close-knit group. When I got married at 22, he was in short pants! Yes, it was a big age gap but it didn't seem to matter.

Looking back now, when I signed for Saints perhaps I regret not asking him what he thought. I just made the decision and didn't really think about how he would have taken it. I suppose when I left, it meant he was on his own at a young age and he would have been upset. But I know he supported my career up north so I expect he would have backed me.

When growing up it's fair to say we didn't have any money, but we survived. Like most families whenever we needed something, mum and dad found the money somehow. As I started to play rugby more, whenever I went away and needed kit, they always managed to buy it and I never wanted for anything on that score.

My mum, Katherine Margaret, who was known as Kitty, was good, very kind and sometimes a little bit too kind. When I was 10 I cut my leg playing by a quarry and because I was bleeding so much, she carried me on her back down to the doctor so he could put stitches in me. She carried me all the way down and back up the hill.

When Basil Lowe and Lionel Swift came down from St Helens to tempt me into signing, my mum had food at the table and a few glasses of whisky for them. She ran the house whilst my dad went out to work. Rhys Thomas, or RT, as his friends called him, was a frustrated farmer as he thought the lawn was wasted land, so we sowed vegetables and had fouls, chickens and even two sows at one stage. I had to feed and swill them down before going to school in the morning.

Mum was the hub of everything and that continued when my kids travelled down to see her—she loved my kids. Dad killed a chicken and mum plucked and cooked it. The kids picked the veg and we all cooked it. There was always lots of baked bread and it was bloody brilliant.

My dad was a great man. He was older than my mum and when he was in his pomp he would go to fairs and fetes in other villages on a Saturday, win the tug of war, collect the two bob prize money, down five pints of beer and then walk back. In 1937, he won two tug of war trophies and he always used to talk about that day. The only team that used to beat his team were Pontypool police…but he gave them a 'good pull' as the saying used to go.

Both mum and dad supported me in anything I did. Dad came to the games as much as he could but my mother hardly came, if at all. Keri and my cousins travelled up north but I think my mother only saw one game at St Helens where I kicked the winning goal from touch to beat Hull. I couldn't have planned it better!

Although I could see the coast from my back bedroom, we had the odd fortnight's holiday in Blackpool. Dad took a party load up there, we travelled by coach and the adults enjoyed a few beers along the way. My auntie lived in a pub down the bottom of the road called The Ship and she would sort us out a keg or two so it always took ages to get to Blackpool. On the way there we always stopped at a pub in Neath and I was probably fairly young when I tried my first pint. In Blackpool we stayed at 66 Withnall Road with Mrs Ample. One of the chaps from the coach, Jimmy John, ended up marrying her. That's just one of the ways we got to know the community in Blackpool! They were good times and extravagant holidays.

Chapel was another big part of my life. At the end of the garden, past the veggies was a road, cemetery and then a chapel. When the house windows were open we could hear singing from the service. I went to chapel as a young lad but don't attend now.

The chapel was the nearest building to my house and every time I went down the road, I had to pass it. When I came home in the evening, on passing the cemetery, I was frightened sometimes. The lamp posts didn't always work either. When you're young, this sort of thing plays on your mind.

As a kid I went to chapel three times on a Sunday but I'm not sure whether it taught me anything. I would go and say verse, and then go again at night to meet the lads. It ended up being more of a social thing as there was nothing else to do. I suppose I spread my wings a little bit when I started playing rugby in Llanelli. Coming north after this upbringing, I could be forgiven for being a little naïve. Some people say I turned my back on Wales and all this tradition when I came up to St Helens but that is rubbish. I loved it then and still do now.

I was born on 14 January 1942 and went to Llywnhendy Primary School, which was a fair walk from my home. I could have gone down one road to that school or to Bynea, but my folks chose the first one. Keri went to Bynea. I didn't play rugby at primary school, just a bit of cricket and possibly a little bit of football. It was a Welsh-speaking school and we studied a bit of English in lessons. I was brought up speaking Welsh at home and at chapel and I don't speak it as much as I used to or as often as I should now.

When I became the manager of the Wales rugby league team in the nineties, I bought Welsh books to catch up and provoke some thought. I certainly understand why people say it is a hard language to learn. Although it was my first language so to speak, I find it difficult now until I hear a bit and it comes back. When I left Llywnhendy there was no 11-plus or anything like that for me. I went to a meeting with one of my teachers, Trevor Jones, at the school and he said: 'There's no point you taking the 11-plus Coslett. I think you should just go to Coleshill. Don't put yourself under too much pressure.' How well he must have known me!

I can honestly say that I never failed my 11-plus…because I never took it. If I hadn't taken the advice and had passed the exam, would I have been at Saints? Who knows, I have been lucky. People have always showed me the right way. He must have seen something that said 'This lad is no good'.

I may have hinted here that I really wasn't academic at all, so for me sport was everything. My favourite subject was Cowboys and Indians and I used to go to the pictures and watch westerns! I just plodded away at school whilst Keri was the clever one!

I didn't start playing rugby at Coleshill Secondary Modern until I was 13 or 14 and I also got my first cap for the Welsh Schoolboys under 15s. I captained the side and when I look in the yearbook, all the other captains came from grammar schools whereas I came from a modern. That gave me a boost and I suppose you could say it was my claim to fame!

Coleshill has been knocked down now but was a typical school building. Dirty brick and lots of kids. It was split into a girls' school and a boys' school and, no; I had no success with the girls either! The boys were at the top of the school and the girls were below so we walked around the railings at breaks and chatted. The lads were outside and the girls were inside…but no, that didn't happen for me!

My sports master Mervyn Bowen was a top man. He always encouraged me and drove me forward. He played for Llanelli as a winger and I can't have enough praise for him. He had me and Jackie Jenkins—the team's half backs from the same form— passing and kicking every afternoon as a scrum half and stand off partnership. It was brilliant. Coleshill beat everyone and I suppose that's what led me to be picked for Wales as captain against Scotland and France. I remember not having a passport for travelling to France and I had a major panic to sort out a picture. I also remember when I got changed for the game noticing that most of my teammates had kit bags. All my kit was stuffed as neatly as possible in a satchel. When I mentioned it to my mum, she said, 'Why not use my shopping bag?'

I said, 'I can't use this mum,' trying to be as nice as possible so I didn't hurt her feelings as I thought my bag was okay. But she insisted. In my next game, I took my kit in mum's bag and straight away Mervyn asked where I got it from. I told him and he said: 'That's good; the last time I saw that bag it was full of bottles of brown ale!' It turned out that Dad had been on the train with Mervyn to support me in Scotland and he was very impressed with the bag's capacity for holding things. My career blossomed from then on as I even had my own kit bag.

Mr Brace was my geography teacher and he was on the committee of Llanelli Schoolboys' Rugby Union Team. I had Mr Morgan for maths and Mr Williams for history and they must have realised I wasn't all that clever, but then again, I wasn't dull either. So they left me to it most of the time. I behaved myself at school; just kept my head down and quietly loved my rugby. I didn't like doing homework, of course, but I reckon the teachers were clued up enough to think 'There's no point pushing this lad, as there's nothing academic there!'

I probably played my first serious game of rugby for the school and Llanelli when I was 13. I had a rugby-heavy schedule which meant training in the afternoon with school, training twice with the town and playing games for both school and the town. My mum must have spent her entire life cleaning my kit!

Once I remember taking my kit home after a game on a Saturday. My mum spent ages washing and ironing it, as she would normally do. The grammar school teacher Mr Thomas saw my kit during the week and he bellowed that I had brought the kit in, un-ironed. I said that my mum would not have sent it back un-ironed. Mum was always spot on with that sort of thing. So I didn't like him for a while. Whether I rumpled it up during the day I don't know. Mum was as unhappy as I was about this and told me I wasn't to play for him again. I was a bit unhappier about that, but it didn't last long.

All in all I had a happy time at school and used to play a bit of cricket in the summer too. You can see why I didn't go to the grammar school though; I played too much sport. As kids, we always played whenever we got the chance and I knew that whatever happened, I would continue playing sport in some form. When I left school at 15, I was offered two jobs. One job was to work in the brewery bottling plant at Buckley's Brewery in Llanelli and the other job was to work in Murray Street in Llanelli as an apprentice mechanic. But the mechanic's job meant I had to go to night school on a Tuesday and Thursday and that wouldn't correspond with my training. So I went to the brewery. That's how much rugby influenced me. Okay, it could have been the thought of night school that put me off. But thinking about it now, I could have been a mechanic after 10 years. I was in the brewery bottling plant, on the wagons and in the brew house. When I signed for Aberavon I was offered a job as a steelworker at the steelworks in Port Talbot. Although the job was further away, it was better money than the brew house.

I was about 13 when I got involved in rugby for the first time. I was picked for my form, then the school and then the town's schoolboys' team. Because of my size I was chosen as stand off, but later played fullback—the position I joined Saints at—in my first game for Llanelli Schoolboys against lads of 15-years-old.

My first game for the town was against Barry and I kicked a penalty goal in a 3–3 draw. I often wondered why I was 13 and these guys were 15 and I was kicking the goals…you would have thought they would have had a kicker older than me. Of course

I was a little overawed at first. There was a good two years' difference between me, the rest of my team and Barry. I thought throughout the game that the lads were much bigger than me! Also I was playing in Barry, around 50 miles from where I lived so the game was a big thing. I was concerned about what was going to happen and I was glad when we drew.

To play for Coleshill and to be selected for the town team was a real honour. The selectors obviously had a little bit of faith in me to give me a start. The selection process was simple—they watched schools in the area and chose the best players from them. At 13 I played at fullback and switched to stand off for the next two years.

In one game for the town we played against Caerphilly, I remember the crossbar coming away from the posts and hitting David Harris, who was at centre, slap bang on the head. We were winning quite comfortably, running the ball from behind our own sticks and suddenly the crossbar fell on his head. Thinking about it now, I suppose it was frightening for him. The posts were timber in those days so perhaps he was lucky. Maybe it knocked a bit of sense into him!

As mentioned earlier, the people who selected me for the schoolboy's team were also on the committee at Llanelli. So when I did move up, I knew the committee at Llanelli and they obviously knew me and what I was capable of. For that reason, I only have admiration for the teachers who kept an eye on me throughout my school days. They put me on the road with plenty of good advice and made me what I am today.

One way we repaid the teachers who had stood by us was to win the Llanelli and District Schools' Rugby Union Dewar Shield two years in a row. Getting to the final of the cup competition, which pitched schoolboy teams against others from all around the area, was like going to Wembley for the Challenge

Cup. That's how big it was. I was lucky enough to play in the team twice. In 1955–56 we beat Cardiff Schoolboys 19–8 over two legs. It was a good game where their forwards got on top but we stuck with it and pulled away after half time. The year after we thrashed Caerphilly Schoolboys and I scored four tries and kicked two conversions. In that year we also scored something like 516 points in our 24 games and only lost one.

I played in those games as stand off after starting out at age 13 as fullback. A stand off player dictates the game. Then I moved back to fullback when I played for Llanelli youth at 15. I was always tall—around 5ft 11 and that was possibly the reason I moved to fullback. Also, I wasn't fast; I didn't have much pace. In effect I'd gone from dictating at stand off, to being a fullback who was dictated to! I didn't get smashed about on the field, but I had to have my wits about me—especially when playing my first game at fullback.

After leaving school at 15, I was picked for the Welsh youth team to play France and England. A year later I was picked again. In the third year just as I thought I was getting better, they dropped me…When I was young, I didn't think too far ahead because I was in the swing of things. I played for my school, town and country at a particular level, then the level or grade changed and I had to start again. To play for Wales Youth and not be picked for the third year; well, it brings a player back down to earth doesn't it? It tells you that when things are going well, they can change at a shot and you have to adapt too.

When you move up a grade after you have been at the 'top' of another, people always look for the mistakes before the goodness. It is up to you to learn from the mistakes. It is always about proving yourself. I took that blow as if I was moving a grade; I had to prove myself to another set of people. Whether getting dropped from the youth was the wakeup call I needed or not, I don't know.

I know they picked Ray Clarke from Hendy ahead of me for a potential record-breaking cap haul. Although I wasn't glad at the time, looking back I am happy for him because he died a young man. I ended up with four caps and he died a happy man because he played for the Welsh youth with two caps. Whilst he is sadly missed, it makes me feel happy to know he has that honour.

I suppose the kids of today have it ever so slightly different with academies and such. They know that if they work hard and are established into a system then they are likely to have a career that will probably pay them well. Rugby back then wasn't like that. We had a couple of bob for expenses and when I played for Aberavon I caught two buses or a train and a bus and to get there. Buses finished at 10 p.m. at night and sometimes I wasn't ready to go home. The club would put on a taxi for me to go home and it was a long way from Port Talbot to Llanelli! Mr Hopkins was on call for me 24 hours a day to send over a driver in his big Humber Hawk to taxi me home. Glyn Overton, the secretary back then, would often say: 'That bloody Coslett again, we can't afford him. Every time he comes he goes home in a taxi.'

But I never thought of the future at all when I was a kid. You could say rugby was just a hobby I suppose. I was brought up playing rugby from 13 and it was just in my calendar, something I did. I was serious but never expected to make anything out of it. When I signed up north, I wasn't seeking a career; the signing meant I had a couple of extra bob to get a deposit on a house, or gave me extra pocket money. There wasn't much money in the game those days—we were all part time. We had enough money to afford a decent holiday and have a bit of pocket money. I never thought ahead and certainly never thought my involvement in rugby would continue for 18 years. I think players earn a little bit more now eh? In those days, we were only paid when we played. This meant that if you had an injury that lasted a few months, and affected your other job, you had no income at all. If you had a family, an injury would make life extremely difficult indeed.

3

'DON'T FORGET YOUR BOOTS. YOU'RE TRAINING...'

Terry Davies was one of the biggest influences on my life as I was coming through school and breaking into Llanelli's youth team. He was a village lad who I looked up to because he was a Welsh international and had bags of experience to boot. Put simply, he was my idol.

When I was young I trained on a farmer's field with Alan Rees, the farmer's son. He was older than me and also played for Llanelli Schoolboys. We lined up kicks and sent them through the window at the top of a barn. I say window...it was a hole about the size of a bale of straw where there was a large pulley. We could do that all afternoon and more often than not, the ball sailed through.

I knew, as did everyone else in the village, that Terry was having a great career for Llanelli and he always took interest in the village's young players coming through. Terry's dad and my dad went to Bynea British Legion on a Sunday night where they'd play bingo, watch a concert or whatever. When I got home from playing for school one night, my dad said: 'Terry wants you to be at his house at 6 p.m. on Tuesday. Don't forget your boots. You're going training with him at Llanelli.'

Terry played for Swansea, Llanelli, Barbarians, Wales and the Lions. How good was that? Being asked to go to his house when I was 16…it was superb and he taught me a lot. We looked at my kicking style, the correct way of tackling and even at how to run correctly. It was fantastic—a real dream come true. He had a car so he took me to train with Llanelli, alongside other household names like Carwyn James. I trained with Llanelli from age 16 and played for their youth team. I remember that I turned 18 on a Thursday and became eligible to play for the first team. The following Saturday I played my first game for the first team.

That first game was against Abertillery on 16 January 1960 and I played fullback. That was Terry's position and I think he played at centre instead. It was absolutely brilliant. I played against the likes of Alun Pask and Haydn Morgan—full international and quality players. It was very daunting too and I kicked a few penalties in a good win.

Did Terry's influence get me a start in the team? I'm not sure. I trained with them and played with the youth team, but obviously the step up from the youth team to first grade rugby is big. They must have thought I had enough ability to go straight into the first team and from there I have never looked back. I felt part of it, though was probably a little nervous, but no one tried to put me out of my place. The team just accepted that I was a first team squad player from day one and I enjoyed it.

I was lucky as I had only played a handful of games for Bynea because I was playing first grade for Llanelli. I wanted to play more often for my village but I'm sure most people would understand why I didn't. In the 1959–60 season, I played 10 games for Llanelli and scored 63 points. A season later I played three times and notched seven points.

I think I had a good season for Llanelli but when we came to play the big games against the likes of Pontypool or any of the big English teams, Terry wanted to play fullback and I moved to centre. So take a game against Pontypool for example, I would be up against Malcolm Price who was a Welsh international and when I faced Northampton I would be up against the likes of Jeff Butterfield who was an English international. I thought I might be catching the short straw, as every time I played centre I came up against some of the world's best internationals.

But it was an awesome and enjoyable experience. At that time, centres were pretty big and just starting to take the ball in, create a maul and start the second phase. Rugby union has followed that pattern ever since. I liked to take the ball in fast, create some space and then the second phase could begin for the rest of the team to feed off.

In 1960, I played against London Welsh in London at fullback in what turned out to be my penultimate game for the club. After the game, Llanelli secretary Arthur Davies said that Aberavon wanted me to play for them. I asked him what he thought and he said it would be a good thing to do. The idea was to go over there, learn my trade and come back to Llanelli the season after. That would most likely happen when Terry had retired though and in the 'transfer' letter they sent to me, it indicated that was their thinking too.

There are a lot of doubters who think Llanelli got rid of me but recently I found some letters which stated I was a Llanelli boy and that they had every intention of signing me when I returned to the club. And to be honest with you, it was the best thing that could have happened to me. My two seasons at Aberavon RU were the last pieces of the jigsaw and a great education. I have never known a team to have more spirit or a set of lads who wanted to play for each other more than that Aberavon team.

I never had any doubts that I wanted to go to Aberavon. I suppose deep down I believed that Llanelli were right in their reasoning for wanting me to go. They thought it was the right thing and Terry thought so too. One of us was playing centre every week when both of our positions at the time were fullback; so it really was the right decision.

I had known the committee at Llanelli since my schoolboy days and they would never have given me duff advice. They weren't thinking of themselves or Aberavon, but the right thing for me. Of course I was disappointed that I wouldn't be playing for Llanelli but I knew if I wanted to play fullback every Saturday that realistically I would have to go elsewhere.

Did I have any doubts? I suppose I was joining a team that wasn't regarded as one of the big four of Welsh Rugby—Llanelli, Cardiff, Newport and Swansea—but I couldn't have cared less about the records; it was just a team that were offering me the chance to play first class rugby. In fact, it was a great honour and a fantastic feeling to know they wanted me in the first place.

When I joined the club in 1960, I was the only 'outsider'. The rest of the players were all locals coming from Port Talbot or the outlying districts, and I was the only player from Bynea, some 30 miles away. I never felt like an outcast and they accepted me straight away. It was important for me to do well of course, but I knew if I did well, then the team probably would too.

My last game for Llanelli was on 19 September against, ironically, Aberavon. I kicked a penalty in a three all draw. Three days later I played 'on permit' (on loan in other words) for Aberavon in a 9–3 win against Aberavon Quins. A further two days later, I officially played my first game as an Aberavon player. It wasn't a dream start. We lost to Cardiff 9–6 at our Talbot Athletic Ground home and going down to them wasn't a great thing. I wondered whether I had done the right thing as I missed a couple of goals—kicking one—but things got better and we kicked on from there. We never lost a game when I played after that.

Despite not winning anything for a long time, Aberavon were a good, if not great, team. They had established players like Cliff Ashton, John Collins, Len Cunningham, Rhys Loveluck, captain Rory O'Connor, Tony O'Connor and Peter Jones. Some of these boys were internationals. John Collins was a pacey winger who was capped 10 times for Wales. He does say that he was capped once for ability and nine times because he could play the piano! He recently called me to say that he would be attending the Aberavon reunion because they needed a piano player. I recall that when I played for Llanelli, playing away against Aberavon was always hard, but I didn't mind playing them at home.

Anyway, whether I was the last piece of the jigsaw and everyone blended together after I joined the team, I don't know. But we were the first Aberavon side to win the Welsh Championship. We didn't have a big squad—just 20 players of which 17 or 18 would play regularly. There were no subs and I think one of the reasons we had such a successful season was because we played together week in, week out. Like any good team we knew each other's strengths and we played to them.

Because of that, we went to places like Bath and became the first Aberavon team to win there in nearly 35 years. We also beat Cardiff 12–6 at Cardiff Arms Park on 11 February 1961 where I kicked two penalties. We were the first Welsh club to win there during the season and it was at that point we realised something might be on.

A fortnight later I notched a century of points in an 18–0 win over Gloucester in our 31st victory of the season. Effectively we won the championship when we beat Llanelli on 28 March. We then secured the title by beating our closest rivals, Bridgend,

12–6. We finished top, winning 40 from 48 and drawing just four. It was nice to go into a good side, and if I helped them become a better side, then I am grateful for that. Going to play for them was a tremendous feeling. Of course we weren't sure winning week in, week out, but we knew we had a good chance and that it would take a good side to beat us.

One thing I also enjoyed was the after game socials. I got to know my teammates really well...but there was always the problem of getting home. I had to catch two buses and a train. I didn't want to go home too early so I called on Mr Hopkins week after week. At first it was only now and then, but the more established with the club I became, the more regular it became...and the more upset the club's treasurer became!

I broke the club's points scoring record that Championship winning season with 188 and, more importantly for me at the time, we played Llanelli three or four times and I'm not sure if we lost to them. The first time we played, we drew, and that's when I felt I might have done the right thing to come and ply my trade. I knew then that Aberavon were a good side. And when we beat Cardiff at Cardiff, people began to believe we could win the Championship. Other towns thought we didn't have the right to win the Championship because we weren't big enough. I think it tells you how good the team was.

For the record, the team I played with to win the Welsh Championship were Alan Bamsey, Bryan Jones, Cliff Ashton, Cyril Jones, Dave Owen, Dave Thomas, Dennis Perry, Ieuan Prosser, Jim Evans, John Bamsey, John Collins, Ken Thomas, Len Cunningham, Owen Hughes, Peter Jones, Phil Morgan, Rhys Loveluck, Roger Michaelson, Rory O'Connor and Tony O'Connor.

One of my overriding memories of appearing for Aberavon is when I returned from a Captain Crawshay select XV game. John

Collins and I were selected in a team of Welsh 'Barbarians' to play on a two game tour of Devon and Cornwall. The Captain Crawshay team were selected from players who were either present internationals or who were possible internationals. The only criteria were that the players chosen had to be in the selectors' minds for the forthcoming Five Nations.

In the first of the two games, on 11 September 1961, we faced Devonport Services and Plymouth Albion and won 25–0. Two days later, on Bank Holiday Monday, we played Camborne and beat them 24–17. John and I had to leave the next day as we were named in the Aberavon team to play Swansea.

To be there in time, we had to catch the 5.30 a.m. train from St Ives, change at Truro and then get to Swansea. As John was the experienced player, he was in charge of the transport plans. So we caught the train, jumped off at Truro only to catch a train departing for St Ives! We got to Swansea at around 7.30 p.m., not long before kick off. As we made our way to the changing rooms the treasurer said: 'Collins, you go and get changed, Coslett, we don't need you, we have a player changed instead of you.'

I was upset and shocked. I thought, 'What am I going to do now?' I didn't want to go into the dressing room so I walked out and tried to weigh up whether to go home without telling them or what. That was my first upset with them. I had been there for three or four minutes when one of the lads came out and said they'd had a vote and wanted me to come back and get changed. The fella who would have been in my place—Glenn Landeg from Bridgend—had been part of the meeting and they all said that 'If one can change, the other can change'. That gave me a tremendous boost and I realised how close as a team we were.

The conditions during the game were horrible—drizzle, wind, cold and, as luck would have it, I kicked a couple of goals and we won 8–3. I kicked a goal from around 50 yards on the touchline and that put us out of sight. It was a bit of a quagmire and I decided I would have a go at anything we were given in the opponents' half. It was heavy, the floodlights were on—but the team weren't great—the crowd booed and gave it to me as they thought I was wasting time. I was really. I took ages to dig a hole, put the ball on top of a pulpit, line myself up and then whack. The ball was leather and soaked through. I still think to this day that if the posts had been 10 yards further back it still would have gone over. With a score of 8–3, it was game over! It was very disappointing to travel all that way to be told I couldn't play. I don't know who was shocked about the goal though, the crowd or me!

I suppose you could say the treasurer was a 'committee man'. He was someone who made a decision without knowing exactly what was going on around him. It's something I won't forget and it was a disappointing time. But, I played, did all right and with that goal thanked the players for the faith they held with me. I was delighted with how I was accepted into the Aberavon family and this incident justified the choice I made in going there.

When I wasn't playing I worked in Port Talbot steelworks on a 6 a.m. to 2 p.m. shift. On match day I would finish a little early, go to Lord and Lady Heycock's house, have a bit of pie, chips and peas and then go to the game. They were brilliant with me. Lord Heycock was also the president of the club and a few days before I signed for Saints, they presented me with a massive wall clock in recognition for my Welsh cap. As he presented it to me he said: 'With great expense again [nodding to me] we present Kelvin Coslett with this wall clock.' I accepted the gift as I didn't know what lay ahead.

I took the clock home and my mum loved it. When I signed for Saints a few days later, the first thing Lord Heycock asked was whether I would be returning the wall clock! I still have it on my wall at home.

4

'I NOTICED A PAIR OF BOOTS ATTACHED TO A PLAYER WHO WAS FLAT OUT ON THE GRASS...'

I suppose when I was selected for the Crawshay XV tour to Devon and Cornwall I knew I had a chance of earning an international cap. It was difficult for me to think about that during the season at Aberavon, as I was only 19 and having a great year. But, I suppose, with the trial games coming, I was in the mix. Whilst on Aberavon's tour to Devon and Cornwall in 1961, I was shocked and delighted when I was chosen to be reserve for the upcoming Wales v France in Paris. Unsurprisingly, Terry was picked as fullback and I would be his reserve...once again.

All the talk leading up to the game was about Terry, and the lads teased me suggesting that as we were both village boys, and that he'd coached and trained me, he would cry off. At that time, Terry and I used to train on a farmer's field in Bynea and they brought the cameras down to film the young apprentice and the master. We were on our haunches having our pictures taken and he whispered in my ear: 'You know I am not pulling out don't you? If you're going to get picked for Wales then you have to earn it. I'm playing.' I thought well that's the fairness of the man. I'm sure he must have sneaked on the bus with us and heard the lads talking!

Terry had around 20 caps for Wales and was an established international. Despite what my teammates said, why should he step down? It is a great honour to play for your country and from day one he told me he was playing. Had I been in his position, I don't think I could have dropped out. But, travelling with the Welsh team was a tremendous experience. I hadn't been out of Llanelli to be honest, so I was learning discipline and growing up. I wasn't disappointed not to be playing—I still found it a thrill to be considered, let alone chosen. I was always under Terry's wing and to be selected as a reserve under him was exciting.

Anyway, France beat Wales but it was a superb trip. Who would have thought that as a kid of 19 I would go up the Champs-Élysées and see the Pigalle? We were restricted as to what we could do though as we had to do exactly the same as the rest of the team just in case something happened to another player. The focus was on the game. We went to a show on the Friday night at the Moulin Rouge and then straight back to the hotel. If I'm being honest, I wanted to fly in, get the game over with and come straight home—after a Parisian banquet of course. Ironically, we got hammered during the game as well as getting hammered at night! The French were hospitable and overall it was an enjoyable experience.

As Terry was retiring the season after and because I was his reserve, people automatically thought I would go into the Welsh team. But of course it doesn't always happen like that. There was a lot of competition and despite winning the Championship the season before, Aberavon weren't one of the top class sides in Wales. Neath, Pontypool and Cardiff all had world-class fullbacks vying for the spot and whilst most people thought I was going to get the spot, traditionally, international players came from those teams.

If I thought I would be a natural successor and walk straight in, then I was clutching at straws. I know I never matched the highs of that 188-point season but I thought, as I had been a reserve for the trip to Wales, and if I could maintain my form, I could be in the mix. It was good they had trials back then so I could show everyone what I could do. This meant I also played against people who were vying for my place. In the end players were selected for Wales solely if they had earned it. I played in all three trials and in the third probables v possibles game I had a particularly bad time with the boot, missing seven chances. Tony O'Connor came over, had a chat with me and said: 'Don't worry about things.' Sod's law, after that I kicked one. It was like he had kicked it for me. We won 20–9. The trials made me think I could do a job for Wales. I suppose I realised I could do it when I was a reserve to Terry—much like when I joined Llanelli. And when I found out I would get a cap, it was a superb feeling.

The squad was announced on the Tuesday night, a week-and-a-half before the first game of the Five Nations. I was on my way to training when I passed an advertising board near a newsagent in Port Talbot and it said something like 'Seven Aberavon Players for Wales'. I thought, 'Now it must be me I must be in with a chance'. I couldn't get to Aberavon fast enough to find out. When I found out for sure, panic set in and training was very entertaining as I could hardly carry or kick a ball. Getting chosen for Wales and picking up a cap was a village event. Bynea and the surrounding villages were really happy and understandably my mum and dad were very proud. Everyone follows Wales in rugby and when one of 'their own' plays for the country it doesn't get any better.

The first Five Nations game was against England at

Twickenham on 20 January 1962 and Aberavon were playing on the Saturday before. In those days, we didn't play the week before just in case we were injured. It was a nervy time just hanging around. One of the things I was most nervous about was that I needed a dinner suit for the after match reception at the Grosvenor Hotel in London.

I deliberated about where to get one and discovered it cost three guineas to hire one. Just when I should have been preparing for my Wales' debut I was panicking about getting a bloody suit. I arranged to hire a suit and took the receipt to Bill Clements, the secretary, and he said: 'Three pounds enough?' I showed him the receipt and he said, yes, £3 would be enough so I ended up losing three bob too. Who was I to argue with him? I was only a kid who had come onto new territory! I found it strange that I would have to wear a dinner suit after seeing people in dinner suits on the telly. It made me feel important. There were no clip on ties in those days either so we had to do up each other's ties after the game.

My first experience of international rugby was travelling to Paris as Terry's understudy where I soaked in the sights and sounds. I should probably have been ready for, or at least expected, what would happen when I played at Twickenham. The team caught the train down a couple of nights before and ended up at the Palladium on the Friday night watching the top billing Charlie Drake Show. There were no coaches as such in those days; it was really committee people telling players what to do and the players then formulated the moves themselves. We had a run around either the day before or on the morning of the match to get our eye in, so to speak.

I can't say I was nervous when I woke up on the Saturday, but at breakfast and looking at the players I could see their anticipation. When we got on the coach to go to Twickenham it built up from there and by the time we arrived at the ground, I couldn't help but be taken in by the whole occasion. The dressing rooms were massive and once we were in them, we wanted to be out playing. Before I went out, Ron Lewis, the masseur, presented me with my shirt and gave me a couple of words of wisdom. That made me feel like the most important person alive.

I still remember lining up in the tunnel like it was yesterday and the wall of noise that hit me from 60,000 Englishman—and a few Welsh, including my dad—as I walked out. The crowd was very noisy and quite clearly they wanted Welsh blood!

The game took a bit to get started as we were presented to the dignitaries and then the National Anthems were played. In the days before the game, I remember Terry saying that being an international fullback was a lot different to playing fullback for club rugby. He said it was faster and as a result you needed to give yourself a couple of yards to plant and position yourself to do the job. He said you have to cover both touchlines and remember to push players onto their least favourite foot to tackle them. That bit of advice was tremendous for me and it certainly kept me on the ball.

Before the game we had to make a late change with Alun Pask coming in for David Nash, proving that being a reserve can land you with a cap if someone is unlucky. But that didn't affect our spirits, as Alun was a top player.

As for the game, well, they always say you should enjoy the moment and I did in so many ways. The game went by a lot faster than club rugby and I had five shots at goal but missed. My style was to dig a hole, pile up the mud and kick off that. But I suppose my boots weren't on my side that day and I kept drifting them wide. The problem with kicking at Twickenham in those days was the gaps between the stands. The wind swirled around the stadium as a result and that made long range kicking more difficult. With the seconds counting down, the game—a real classic—was tied nil apiece and I felt I had done okay throughout. I dealt well with Richard Sharp who had done Wales for pace on a number of occasions and just wanted to keep the ball in their end.

But as the referee moved to blow his whistle, Budge (Buzz) Rogers flew down the wing and kicked over my head. As he kicked, I went towards him hoping to charge the ball down. But he carried on coming and we collided. He happened to run into my shoulder and I suppose, on reflection, I certainly caught him well. He kicked it and it seemed to be a long time before we collided. I don't really know whether he caught his head with my shoulder.

I remember the whistle going and John Curry—one of England's bigger second rowers—leaning over me, he wasn't a happy bunny. But Buzz hadn't scored and it finished 0–0. After the whistle the National Anthems piped up again and as I looked to my left, during 'God Save Our Queen', I noticed a pair of boots attached to a player who was flat out on the grass. To this day I am very unimpressed that Buzz didn't stand up for the anthems...

Going back to club rugby after an international is always a bit of a letdown but I had a job to do at Aberavon. We played Pontypool a week before our clash with Scotland in Cardiff and I was doing pretty well until Benny Jones smashed my nose. That brought me down to earth pretty quickly as I realised I may have to miss the international. There was talk that I may have to wear some sort of mask but I knew I was going to play. They would have had to drop me to do that. It was the first time I had broken my nose although it has been broken many times since.

In Cardiff, conditions were awful but I was looking forward to playing in front of my home crowd. The changing rooms were in the North Stand but for some reason we had to walk to the South Stand, through the crowd, and run out onto the pitch from there. All the teams came out of that end and I still don't understand why. I suppose it was a little bit of theatre that built up the excitement for when the players entered the field.

Scotland hadn't won at Cardiff for nearly 27 years but they had a good team with the likes of Arthur Smith and Gordon Wardle and they certainly looked capable of causing an upset. We played against the wind and rain in the first half and Scotland ran in two tries. They might have been my fault; whether my clearance kicking wasn't up to scratch I don't know; I'll leave the analysis to the so-called experts. In the end, Wales lost 8–3.

In the days after the game I was understandably disappointed. Kicking in the type of conditions during that game was my strength—as I proved in Swansea—and it did make me question when my form was going to return. Perhaps I was blaming the conditions at Twickenham and Cardiff too much? Even some of the Aberavon supporters asked what happened with the kicks. These comments hurt as in my view I had an okay game. I did wonder if I was going to be dropped for the Ireland game. As it happens I was picked for that game, but it was called off due to a foot-and-mouth outbreak.

Thankfully, three weeks later, the selectors stuck with me again and I repaid them in spades. France were Five Nations Champions but were determined to end their campaign in Cardiff on a real high. A smallpox scare in Wales had reduced the crowd to around 50,000, but the atmosphere was just as good. I was once again selected at fullback and decided to attempt pretty much every kick opportunity that came my way. I'm surprised, even in modern rugby league, that players don't attempt more penalty kicks instead of running the ball. The opposition have to claw those points back and it is a psychological advantage. In those days I could kick goals from the half way line and that meant the opposition wasn't going to be hasty in making an indiscretion. It meant they had to play good rugby union. Two penalties earned us six points and that meant the opposition had to score twice. If you had a good side, then that was it because they had to work very hard to get past you.

I had two shots on goal during that game. At my first attempt I finally popped one over and it wasn't an easy goal in the slightest. It was around 35 yards, into the wind, and it sailed over. Talk about feeling relieved. I missed one more kick after that shot but the first kick won the game 3–0 and I repaid the selectors who had total faith in me.

When you're the designated kicker in any side if you miss one, especially one that is all so important, that's all people remember. Look at Don Fox missing that goal in the Challenge Cup Final—that's all people remember. He actually won the Lance Todd Trophy that day and they certainly didn't give it to him because he missed the final kick of the game. The Lance Todd Trophy is chosen 10 minutes before the end of the match but that missed kick is all that people recollect.

Being a kicker brings added responsibility, but was I given my three international caps because of my kicking, or because of my complete capabilities in playing fullback? I thought I was good enough to play for Wales even without my kicking ability. I could kick goals from all over the place for Aberavon; my statistics show that.

When playing against England I took on three from the half way line and the other two from touch. Not many established kickers would even attempt them, but in the records it says I only kicked one in the three games. If you look at it in black and white it questions why I was in the team at all. But didn't I save a try at Twickenham when I 'tackled' Rogers? We could have lost the game, and my intervention saved us from that record.

Was my play good enough, or was it only my kicking that was bad? Because I missed some goals, people say I wasn't as good as others who came along who didn't kick goals. But I kicked the winner against France…or was the game won by the forwards who battled, or by the tackling of the whole team? Johnny Wilkinson takes flack because he misses goals, but isn't he in the team for much more than that? He won the World Cup for England, but his kicking has been off since then and now the press is jumping on their former boy wonder.

I was as disappointed as the rest of the team because we didn't beat England and lost to Scotland. But was my play good enough? Was I good enough to warrant selection without my kicking ability? Would I have been picked if I didn't kick goals? I was finding touch and clearing my lines all through the game—sometimes with kicks of 60 yards—and taking the pressure off the forwards. I certainly didn't have a bad game because I missed a couple of goals. It's not like in American Football where they bring on a kicker to win the game. And, in two of the three games I played in, we nilled the opposition!

I suppose life is full of little disappointments and it's how you pick yourself up from them that makes you the person you are. Unfortunately, I missed out on a 'clean sweep' of caps as the game against Ireland was called off because of foot-and-mouth. But when you say you have played three times in the Five Nations, it puts a question in there as most international players have four caps. Incidentally, after the Five Nations, the powers that be decided to change the rules on time wasting. This was probably because I had taken too long with my goal attempts. They said kicks could only take a maximum of two minutes.

At the end of the season, around June, I was named as reserve to go on the Lions tour to South Africa. That seemed to be the story of my life. First I was reserve to Terry at Llanelli, then reserve for Wales and was now reserve for Tom Kiernan from Ireland and Ken Scotland from Scotland who had been chosen in front of me. I would have played the back row if they had asked! Similar to being the reserve for Wales, I trained hard in case I had to go over and also got measured for a suit.

Unbelievably on the tour, centre David Hewitt got injured and I expected a call to go over there. Instead of paying to fly me over, they called up John Brown who was on a rugby tour with the RAF in South Africa. He played for Blackheath and hadn't even been selected, but ended up with a Lions' Cap. I had been selected as a reserve, trained all summer just in case, then found out in the press the selectors had chosen the cheapest option. I was absolutely gutted and felt cheated out of a place on the tour.

On the other hand, how lucky could Brown get?

5

'BECAME THE OWNER OF ONE NEW AND VERY FEISTY FERRET...'

Rugby league wasn't an alien sport in the valleys. I watched Wigan play at Llanelli in 1958 when they were on a Welsh tour. I watched St Helens against Wigan at Wembley in 1961 on TV and marvelled at Tom Van Vollenhoven and Billy Boston. It was a sport much like union, of course, and I could see plenty of similarities from the position of 'fly half' to league's stand off.

I first knew of the game's interest in me when a scout from Whitehaven appeared at Aberavon, but he didn't say anything. A few weeks later a fella from the Rhonda came down and asked me if I would be interested in going north. I told him that I might be and I would be prepared to listen to what he had to say. To be honest, I wasn't really bothered. I enjoyed union, had a job I liked in Port Talbot and my family were close by. But, a couple of weeks later, the scouts were back.

I had finished my afternoon shift at the steelworks and the work's bus had dropped me off at the bottom of the road. It was 11 p.m. and my cousin's wife Brenda was at the bus stop. She said: 'Hello Kelvin, there's two English men at your mother's...'

That was a strange thing so I ran up the hill to see what was going on. Lionel Swift and Basil Lowe—Director and Secretary from St Helens—had come down to sign me. They sat drinking my mother's whisky and eating sandwiches and wouldn't go until I signed. It was 4 a.m. when they left with my signature and I still wonder whether I put pen to paper because I just wanted them out of the house!

But why did I sign? There was a lot going on in my head back then and I suppose the honest answer was for financial gain and because it just felt right. There was no pressure from my family or Terry. They made it clear it was my decision all along. I knew Llanelli wanted me back and Aberavon wanted me to stay so perhaps St Helens were the excuse I needed not to have to choose between two lots of great people. Perhaps it was the disappointment of not playing for the Lions. I don't know. Looking back, I'm not sure whether I would have done something differently, but I don't regret it in any way. Perhaps I think I should have had a more clear vision of what was in front of me. But hindsight is always a good thing.

After I signed I went to Terry's to tell him what I had done, and maybe I should have spoken to him first. I don't know. He had been made an offer too, so the waters were pretty cloudy when I signed. My folks didn't really want me to go, but they realised it was my life and it was an opportunity to better myself. They wanted it to be my decision.

I was naïve though. Going north was harder than I expected. I didn't realise at the time how important a decision it really was. I mean, what if things hadn't gone right? I played in every game in the first two seasons bar a couple. Who could have guessed my career in the north would go so well? What if I hadn't established myself or got injured? I was lucky that everything went well.

Thinking back now, if something had gone wrong there would have been very little for me to return home to. I only had my job because I played for Aberavon. Would Llanelli or Aberavon really want me back? I'm sure rugby union rules stated I couldn't have gone back anyway. I didn't have a trade. I couldn't really have said, 'Bugger it, I'm off home'. Being at home would have been great, but there was nothing there for me.

The more I think about it, the more of a risk it was I suppose. At least I let down both Llanelli and Aberavon together instead of choosing just one club in preference to the other. It was a difficult decision and in reality the right one in the end.

Was I worried about trying a different sport? I find that people always look for fault anyway! If Saints sign a new player, the fans will spot his mistakes before his worth. This is more apparent if you are a kicker coming from union. Not that I didn't believe in my ability, but I didn't realise what was in front of me. I simply thought I was off to play rugby and that the games would be similar.

I remember playing against Australia and seeing a photograph in a brochure that showed Raper scorching in against us and I am something like five metres away. I had actually just tackled someone, and it shows the picture does lie sometimes. They beat us 8–2 and at the reception at the town hall our Chairman Harry Cook said: 'If our goalkicker [me] had been on form we would have beaten Australia today.' Now, if there has ever been an occasion where someone was called for losing a game, that would be it! If I had been at the club for a while, perhaps he wouldn't have said that. But they signed me as a goalkicker and I suppose if I was not producing the goods then he probably had a right to comment!

Anyway, I signed for Saints on 17 July 1962—something that made *News at 10*—for a decent sum, but I've never told anyone what the figure was and I'm not going to break my silence now. My close family know, but no one else, and I'm sticking to that. It wasn't a great sum however. People think signing on fees are great, but players who move around get more and those who remain faithful to a club can lose out. At the end of the day, union players came into league for financial reasons.

I had to be in St Helens 14 days from the date of signature so there was very little time to think about what I was letting myself in for. I knew Basil Lowe and Stan McCormack would meet me at Lime Street and that the club had sorted me out some digs on Willow Road, just behind the Popular Side at Knowsley Road.

When I arrived at the train station which was three or four miles from my house and saw people from three villages waving me off, I was pretty emotional. They presented me with an electric shaver and wished me all the best. The new job in the north was a gamble really and looking back now I didn't have any plan for moving there. I literally signed for Saints and had to be there 14 days later. There was nothing in the contract to say how long I would play for Saints, and I didn't even know if I would be any good. Physically, I was in great shape as I had been training for the Lions tour, and as I arrived at Saints in July, there would be a couple of months before my first game. Had Saints got me at the right time after all?

Watching the houses and the country rolling by from my train window was a sobering experience. Perhaps I was beginning to understand the enormity of my decision. More likely, it was because I hadn't been away from home that much. When the train pulled into Liverpool Lime Street, I was shattered. The station was packed. Stan McCormack and Basil Lowe were there ready to pick me up. Straight away Stan started calling me Kel as he said Kelvin just wouldn't do. Perhaps it wasn't tough enough for rugby league, I don't know. So as well as having a new home in a new country, I now had a new name, Kel.

Within the first couple of weeks I'd settled in at Willow Road with Mrs Seed, my landlady, being an absolute gem. When I went out she left me a pint of milk and a pie on the table—although most of the time I had to force it down when I got in after a couple of beers. I'd been used to going to chapel three times on a Sunday—more for social reasons as I've said, but there was none of that when I got to St Helens. John Temby, Wilf Smith and I used to go for a pint on a Sunday. It was allowed, as we weren't playing in July!

Imagine my surprise when only two weeks into playing for St Helens, I found myself having a beer at Bold Miners before moving on to Derbyshire Hill Labour Club to play bingo at 2 p.m. This became my new Sunday routine. Only the second time I was in the Labour Club, I looked up and noticed a woman taking her clothes off in front of a load of shouting blokes. I had gone from attending chapel three times a day on a Sunday to sitting in some kind of strip joint! It was some change in the space of two weeks I can tell you and it was a massive education for me! If she'd ever found out, my mum would have killed me.

I'd probably just found my feet in the town when I had my first game of league—a trial against Saints 'A'. I can't remember much about it, but I think I did all right! My first real game, a friendly, was against Liverpool Stanley. We won 33–2 and I kicked six goals and scored a try. Our first league game was at Salford on 18 August 1962 and we beat them 35–24. Vollenhoven got a hat trick that day and I kicked four goals. I then kicked 10 when Salford came to Knowsley Road.

Those early games were a baptism of fire for me and I wanted at least to look like I knew what I was doing. Coming in at fullback meant I replaced Austin Rhodes—who had played in the 1961 Challenge Cup Final. Him and Ken Large started the season, but never actually played a game. When I arrived, both stayed until around September, then left to join Leigh. They were okay with me off the field, but it must have been difficult for them seeing so many new faces come in. Len Killeen and John Temby joined at the same time.

John was a real character—but then again the whole team was made up of real characters. With teammates like Mick Sullivan, Dick Huddart, Cliff Watson, Bob Dagnall, Vollenhoven and Alec Murphy, there was always something going on. Some of the lads were local and others were from South Africa, Cumbria and other places. Our 'A' Team coach Steve Llewellyn was the only Welsh bloke! There were certainly some communication issues early doors! There was Tom Van Vollenhoven from South Africa, Cliff Watson from the Midlands and Bobby Dagnall from St Helens. I was a typical Welsh boy so we had some fun trying to communicate initially.

Apart from being a great winger, Sullivan also got me started on the horse racing game by taking me on a painful trip [wallet wise] to Haydock Racecourse one day and that consistency has continued, as I rarely back a winner these days either! But they all looked after me and as the beers, games and wins flowed I became more comfortable with being at St Helens.

It could have been difficult for me, and of course, there was some resentment that I had been signed by the club—from within—but I really wanted to make a go of it and that season I believe I did just that. I didn't miss a game all year and topped the goal scoring chart, proving to myself and others that I could make it in rugby league. When I arrived at the club I didn't have a car and passing my driving test was proving quite elusive. I tried to keep in touch with my family and friends in Wales but back then it was a difficult journey. I did miss home, but my landlady looked after me and the club were excellent too.

When I hit 21, I met Jacqueline who turned out to be the person to put me on the straight and narrow for the next 40-odd years. Ruskin Drive, where the Saints' first team now trains, was always somewhere to meet for a couple of beers and a dance—especially on a Saturday night.

There were always dances around the town, either at Helena House or in clubs and pubs. On the night I first met Jacqueline, I'd had a couple of jars and had to pass the entrance at Ruskin to go to the toilet. As I wandered past I noticed a girl talking to two lads and I thought to myself 'She's alright'. On my return from the toilet the same girl had five lads surrounding her. I walked straight over and said something like: 'Excuse me, are you dancing?' or 'Would you care for this dance?' in front of the other five lads. There was no turning back at that point. Thinking back now, I couldn't dance either but I must have shown her some good moves…although the beer helped. I don't know who was more shocked, me for asking or her for accepting. I had to give it some small talk too so I guess something must have worked.

Being in digs meant I didn't go out much during the week other than to the pictures. Jacqueline was at night school at the time and now looks after me in my older years! Without meeting Jacqueline, it could have been a very lonely time. When I first arrived at Saints I trained in the morning on my own because I wasn't working. What kept me going was that I was doing well on the field. If I'd gone to Saints and hadn't got a place in the team then it could have been very difficult. That's why I have always made a point of contacting injured players as once injured, players can soon be forgotten. If you don't work, you can get bored as well. When I first arrived at Saints I decided to learn to drive; when I passed it meant I could get back to Wales. Despite this, there came a point when I wanted to work as well. It was hard at the time.

As I didn't do anything else during the week, it made me a little more anxious on match day because I wanted to perform and get stuck in. I was more than glad when Fred Buckley from the highways department in St Helens, and a friend of Basil Lowe, offered me a job driving a dumper. I think that was important at the time as it took my mind off matches as I now had something to do.

Before I got that job, I trained a little on a Monday morning with Dick Huddart who was on the verge of going to Australia. One particular Monday, I had arranged to meet Jacqueline outside the Coach and Horses in Rainhill at 7 p.m. to go to the pictures. I came up to the club to train as usual and Dick was there. We ran about for a bit, then after around three quarters of an hour he asked me what I was up to in the afternoon. I told him I had a date later but that I wasn't doing much otherwise. He suggested we went for a few pints up the 'Abbey' pub.

After hammering the beer there, we went to the Legion or 'The Bloodbath' as it was known in Parr, at 4 p.m. There was a bloke sat at the bar selling ferrets and he spotted a pair of mugs—well, me and Dick—straightaway. He immediately marched over to Dick and said he was flogging ferrets for 10 bob. He then said, straight up, that if Dick could put his finger in the ferret's mouth and take it out without getting bitten, then he could have the ferret for free. Feeling the beer's warm glow, Dick nonchalantly stuck his finger in the ferret's mouth and pulled it out. He then downed his pint in one and became the owner of one new and very feisty ferret.

Suddenly, I realised it was nearly 6.30 p.m. and I had a date at 7 p.m. I finished my beer then said I had to go. But we had the bloody ferret to contend with! Dick asked a chap at the bar if he wanted to buy a ferret for 10 bob. It turned out to be the guy that Dick had just won it from. In the end we had to let the ferret go outside. Of course I turned up late for my date and Jacqueline decided to take me home to meet her mother. What a poor introduction it was to my future mother-in-law—a very drunk Kel smelling of ferrets.

On the field, it didn't take me long to get to know the game. As well as practising kicking through the barn, in Bynea we trained twice a week and played touch rugby instead of scrummaging—effectively the same as rugby league. In training we played the ball and didn't have our heads stuck up someone's arse all day. There was a lot more space in league and I really enjoyed it.

With the position of fullback, I tried to cover what might happen so I would be in the right position. I said to Cliff Watson that the forwards take the ball in for a bit and then have a rest whilst I am at the back—out of the way of everyone—covering the play. I think I may well have been tempting fate as a couple of seasons later when I was struggling to get my place back in the team after breaking my leg, I played in the pack and it was bloody hard work. It was probably my own fault to be honest.

During the 1962–63 season, I played in every game and scored points in all but one. I never expected to be an automatic choice and always looked for my name on the team sheet. On 20 April 1963 we played Featherstone and won 18–5, but I missed six goals and didn't score. Irritatingly that one poor kicking game meant I ruined my otherwise impressive record of scoring and playing in every game that season.

The season was somewhat truncated as there was a cold snap, which wiped out the fixture programme over January and February. We basically trained in Broadway School's gym and on our running track underneath the stand at Knowsley Road for around two months. When we returned, we lost to Hull KR

3–2 away then Halifax beat us in the first round of the Challenge Cup. Losing wasn't great as we battered them. Wilf Smith was going well at scrum half that day until he swapped with Alex Murphy—as usually happened during a game—and Murphy kept hold of the ball thinking he could do it all by himself; he usually could.

Murphy was such an individualist and that Halifax game sticks in my mind. He was 'the' player and everyone told him he was the best. Murphy always played like that. There's no doubt he was a superb world class player, and he believed he could win games by himself. The opposition put him in a cage and tried not to let him play. When he left Saints we'd had a good education on how to stop his game. The older he got the more 'playmaker-like' he became and he brought other players into it.

That season we also travelled to Blackpool to face Blackpool Borough where Bobby Dagnall was flattened and concussed. We stayed in Blackpool for a while and had a few beers, went up in the tower and to see the monkeys. We propped him up in the tower, gave him a few beers and he had a good time. Of course, he didn't have a clue what was going on and I bet his head was bad the next day! Voll drove back that night in a battered old Ford Zephyr after a few beers and that wasn't much fun either. He drove through red lights and everything. I wasn't a keen passenger when he was driving and I have to say it was one of the most frightening experiences of my life.

But Voll was one of those players you could always rely on during a game. If Saints ever had a go-to player, then he would be it. Earlier in the season he was immense as we beat Swinton in the Lancashire Cup Final. Prop forward Jack Arkwright was sent off for fighting with Ron Morgan. It was a good fight too and Jack refused to take a step back—like the rest of his family.

Swinton were a big and formidable team back then and had

a good side with Ron Morgan, Alan Buckley and fullback Ken Gowers who always seemed to be in with a shout of international honours before me. We played the final in October at Central Park in Wigan in torrential rain. It was horrible under foot. Voll went in the corner and I banged over the conversion and a penalty. There was a crowd of about 23,000 that day as it was a real occasion. But Voll's performance was incredible. There was something special about him during that game. It was like he was using Swinton's players to push himself forward.

I earned my first medal in my first season and I was understandably delighted. In fact, the whole season was successful. We finished second in the league—six points behind Swinton—and I scored three tries and 156 goals for 321 points. I was pleased with how my game had come through and that the form I showed with the boot at Aberavon had stuck with me.

A cartoonist called Barton used to taunt me in the press about my kicking style and how I would dig holes on the pitch to get enough mud to put the ball on. I would place the ball on the mud—like a modern day kicking T—and kick the point. Of course, it could take time to get the right mound—especially if the ground wasn't right. The fans would have been calling me of course, but I used to switch off and get myself set. I would put the ball on, eventually, take a few steps back and it seemed to work for me. Barton always made an issue of it though. One of his pictures had molehills all over the place and another was like a construction site. It was a bit sarcastic I thought.

If moving up from Wales wasn't enough that season, I was almost wiped out in a car crash! My employers Basil Lowe and Harry Cook asked me to go down with them to South Wales to have a look at a player they might sign. It turned out to be Dai Watkins who played for Newport. Dai was a stand off, a great player and they simply wanted me to be honest about the club.

On the way back, around Merthyr Tydfil way, Harry was driving and the car seemed to jolt, skidded down an embankment and then careered into a ditch. It turned out he had mistimed a sharp turn in the road. The car flipped onto its side and for a split second Harry and I just looked at each other. Then we decided to get out and noticed Basil had already gone. I tell you, these old fellas don't half shift when they need to! And you know what made it worse? Dai decided to stay in Wales to earn a cap instead of coming north! You can't blame him for that though.

6

'WHEN YOU ARE NOT PLAYING, YOU START TO LOSE CONFIDENCE...'

One thing I realised about Stan McCormack early on was, apart from not liking the name Kelvin, he wasn't a real table banger. He talked a good game and realised that by getting the players on his side, he could get them to do what he wanted.

Being an ex-international winger, he was knowledgeable and had played with great players. He tried to pass on his experience and listen to our opinions. Perhaps people thought he wasn't strong enough and that might have been the reason he was eventually let go, but the players responded to him and we won trophies.

In 1963–64, the club signed some good players as they looked to push on from the season before. Peter Harvey and John Warlow came in, as did Stan Owen and Doug Laughton. Owen was one of those players I was glad was on my side rather than the opposition's. In my first season I played with Cliff Watson who was one of the best forwards in the game and he told me I would have to keep an eye on Stan. After playing against him— he played for Leigh and Rochdale—I realised why. He added

59

real go forward to the team and steel to the pack. He was a leader.

I also played with Stan in February 1963 for Wales when we took on France in Toulouse. The cap made me a dual international and there aren't many of those around. It was the first Welsh rugby league team put together for a while and we wanted to make an impact on Wales and the rest of the league community.

Our only recognised hooker was injured so we had to go with Charlie Winslad who was a prop forward. Owen propped with Ron Morgan and we had Ray Glastonbury and Johnny Freeman on the wing. Leeds' Colin Evans came in, as did Lewis Jones. Lewis was a bit of a golden boy for Wales so it was good to have him in the team.

Without a recognised hooker it was hard to win the ball at the scrum. As a result, France didn't let us have much of the ball and we lost 23–3. That taught me that if you had the ball, then it was difficult to get it back. The French were also ruthless in the pack and if you compare our pack with theirs, it was always going to be a rough game. Owen threw his weight about a lot but didn't get damaged until well after the match. The French were excellent hosts and provided a lot of wine at the post-match dinner. Stan took a tumble, cut his eye open and had to have six stitches. When we got back home reporters saw the wound and called it the 'Battle of Toulouse'. They hadn't been to the game, put two and two together and came up with six stitches.

John Warlow's signing was significant. He was a good friend from back home and having him at St Helens kind of made it easier for me in continuing to adjust to life up north. It was a big thing for him to sign and I thought he was good for the club. He was always quiet and gave his all. I suppose I was a big part of him signing for the Saints. I went to his mum and dad's house to meet him and, like I did with Dai Watkins, gave him my views on St Helens. I was obviously more successful this time.

I told him that the Board were okay; I'd had a good start and I thought things were rosy. I said the people of St Helens were good—much like the people of Llanelli—but said it was a big decision to make and that there was no going back once he'd signed. I told him to get as much money as he could because there wouldn't be another opportunity like it. I suppose that seemed a little mercenary, but they were the things that you needed to think about.

Warlow believed me and signed that night. To celebrate we both showed Harry and Basil how to drink. It's funny thinking about how much we drank back then, but we played and trained hard as well. We played on the Saturday or Sunday and then had a couple afterwards, although we only had a few drinks and only ever drank beer. Youngsters these days drink potent lager that is five or six per cent. In our day we drank mild and that was around 2.4 to 2.8 per cent. This meant we drank over a longer period of time. I believe strong drinks contribute to a breakdown of society and we should remember that today's cider and beer are potent drinks. Therefore we shouldn't drink as much of them. As I said earlier, we just drank mild and enjoyed the occasion. Alcohol marketing has changed however, as the brewing trade used to tell us we couldn't get a better medicine than a pint of mild a day—if we had a blood disorder, then we were supposed to eat yeast! I don't think that would be allowed today!

Led by Stan, our side had real character and it was no surprise that we won some silverware. We beat Leigh at Swinton 15–4 to retain the Lancashire Cup and beat Swinton in the Western Championship Final 10–7. That tie was played at Wigan in front of 17,363 and Ray French scored. Whenever you speak to him about it now, he claims he ran about 50 yards to score, but in reality he ran around five yards! Either way, it was a vital try just beside the post and it put us right back in the game.

When Frenchie went in, Stan McCormack leapt up in the dugouts and cracked his head on the concrete roof. He split his head open and needed five or six stitches! Stan was also one of the first coaches to instil the virtues of water on us. No one listened, but he would get nervous and drink out of the trainer's bucket. God knows what things were in that bucket after the magic sponge had been rubbed over the players but he didn't seem to mind. Sometimes he wouldn't have the patience to get a cup and dived straight in.

Looking back at that 1963–64 season, a return of two trophies and being third in the league, nine points behind Champions Swinton and three behind Wigan, was a good return. But on the way back from the last game of the season—an 11–10 defeat at Castleford—the Board let Stan go. And when I say on the way back, I actually mean on the team bus. We all thought we'd had a decent season and Stan was leading the singing on the bus. He got called to the front seats where the Directors were and was fired. Seriously! There were only a couple of days before the next Board meeting and they could have done it then really. He came to the back of the bus and told us and we laughed. We thought it was a joke and that really took the seriousness off it. You can't win everything all the time and I think people forget that. There will be few worse coaches than Stan. He nurtured me when I came to the club and I was very thankful for that.

Many players undergo second season syndrome—where other teams find out about their style and subdue them as a threat. But I seemed to keep on going and that second year was another good one for me. I scored five tries and kicked 138 goals. I'd like to think my run of form proved I was a decent rugby league player and showed people I had made the right choice in coming north. The season after in 1964, I was only three games in when I shattered my leg.

I had started the campaign in really good form—kicking five in Saints' first 'real' game against Leigh and then kicked seven from seven two days later on 24 August against Rochdale. Midway through the second half one of their players broke through, kicked over and the resultant collision snapped my fibula. I had my own system when I was fullback and someone chipped over me. I would watch a player's eyes, put him in a 'pen' so to speak and then whack him. Instead of waiting, this time I decided to meet him straight on. I went over to shoulder charge him and someone came over at the same time and met him. He fell over on my leg and I went over as well. I knew from the snap my leg was broken straight away. Cliff Watson carried me off on his back and they sorted me out off the field.

It was panic stations then because in three weeks time—on 12 September—I was due to marry Jacqueline! After meeting her at Ruskin Drive and her recovering from the 'ferret' day, I popped the question as we were getting along so well. Even so there had been more dodgy dates for her to endure. Before the ferret incident, on either our third or fourth date, we were at the pictures. In the middle of the film, a note came over the screen asking if Mr Kel Coslett would report to the office.

'Isn't that you?' Jacqueline asked. I said I thought it was. She said she would stay watching the film and I left to see what was wrong. I had no idea where the office was but when I found it, Tommy Smith was there looking for Wilf Smith, his brother, who hadn't turned up after a big night out. I said I had no idea where Wilf was! We had a debate about where he had gone, and of course I didn't have a clue! Jacqueline was still waiting in the cinema and I didn't know whether she would still be there when

I returned. I had some explaining to do!

I think getting married was a good thing for me, as I didn't suit digs. Mrs Seed was a little fusspot but looked after me like her own son. It was a good job I liked milk, though. However she also went up to the local butchers—McColls—every day to get fresh meat for me.

Basil Lowe also sussed out Jacqueline too. When I had been courting her for a while he invited us for Sunday tea with his wife just to check her out. We were convinced they were eying her all over and they were probably scared she would lead me astray. So I suppose that led me to marriage pretty easily!

As I had a broken leg, finding a suit to get married in was difficult. Ken Courtman in St Helens provided a decent a pair of trousers and the lady who lived across the road—Mrs Matthew—split the seam and put several hooks and eyes in it. When the plaster cast was off, she undid this and turned it into a normal suit.

I walked down the aisle on crutches, said my vows and we are still together! We got married in St Ann's Church in Rainhill with John Warlow as my best man. On the same day, Saints played Blackpool Borough and a few of the guys came to the wedding black and blue afterwards. A coach load of my friends and family came up from Wales and we had a great reception upstairs in the Alexander pub in Thatto Heath. I went upstairs to the reception but discovered the toilets were downstairs. I had to lean on my crutch on the way downstairs and it was a real pain. A couple of times the crutches flew out of my grasp causing people to duck. For our honeymoon we were supposed to go to Brighton, but there was no way I could drive that far, so we had to cancel it.

When not playing, you start to lose confidence. Joe Coan was an experienced fitness coach back then, which meant we were the most physically prepared team in the league. He had been part of the club under Stan McCormack and was a rugby union coach from Cumberland. Joe inherited a team with bags of talent and he was an excellent conditioner. He was one of the first coaches to concentrate on getting the team fit. Unfortunately, once teams had worked out how to beat us he couldn't teach us to play differently, and we had no moves then.

Initially, he was lucky because he got the team fitter than the rest of the league. As well as this, the team had the ability to play well and could decide how they should play. As a result the club won a lot of games in the last quarter in that season and we steamrollered teams as a result. You have to give credit to Joe for making that happen.

But fitness can only take you so far—when you start to lose you need your coach to get you through. Other clubs were constantly monitoring how to beat us and we couldn't get out of that. Lots of clubs had the ability but were not as fit as the Saints. Joe Coan was one of the first to make sure we were ready for the full 80 minutes.

It's difficult to come back from an injury as you can be long forgotten by the fans, your teammates and the coaching staff. They obviously need to get someone in your place and if the replacement plays well in your absence then it can be a long way back. I'd already had a run in with Joe when he suggested I had flat feet and I think he couldn't wait to get local lad Frankie Barrow into that number one spot. I was out for a while and Frankie hadn't been a first teamer for two years so when I came back he didn't really want to play me.

I had only played twice under Joe so he didn't really get to know what sort of player I was before I broke my leg. That was very frustrating especially when I tried to make a comeback. Being out for so long was bitter sweet. I watched the team perform well, but I'd got married and that was obviously a happy time for me. But niggling away in the back of my mind was the fact that if I'd been out of the game for so long, it would be difficult to become involved again. That's why, even now, I always make sure injured players at the club come to training so they stay involved with the team.

It was different in those days; we only trained twice a week. The rugby club soon forgot players unable to attend training because they couldn't travel or whatever and moved on. In my coaching days I always wanted injured players to be involved somehow because it is a lonely trek back on your own. It is especially difficult coming back from a serious injury like a broken leg or ankle.

People have often asked me, when I've been out of the game injured, if I've ever wanted the player that replaced to me to 'fail' in some way. It's difficult, because you are jealous that they are playing, but I just wanted to play! It wasn't a case of I wanted to come back and have exactly the same role as before. I just wanted to be on the field again regardless of whether I kicked or not.

To demonstrate this, Len Killeen and I joined the club at the same time. I was a more than consistent kicker, chosen for my kicking. When I came back from injury, Len kicked instead and I only took ones that he didn't fancy. Killeen was an athlete. He would have excelled in cricket, baseball and basketball. He had tremendous power, but could be wayward with his kicking. I didn't say: 'I'm playing, I kick goals,' because I just wanted to play. I played scrum half once. It didn't matter to me as long as I was playing somewhere in the team.

Anyway, as was the case back then, when you came back from injury you were pitched into the 'A' Team, or reserves, to get a run out and some game time under your belt. I had been out since 29 August 1964 and began playing again at the beginning of January the following year. I turned out against Liverpool alongside Tom Van Vollenhoven who was recovering from injury as well as John Mantle and we won 17–5. I then played two days later (9 January) against Wigan in Kenny Williams' first game and more than 4,000 people came to watch us win 37–7.

I felt I'd shown enough in the two games to prove I was fit and decided not to play in the 'A' Team anymore as I was ready for first team rugby. Joe wanted me to play in a further game but I refused. I spoke with Chairman Harry Cook about it and my decision went in front of the Board. A couple of days later, they voted three to two that I should play. The first I heard that I was to play against Warrington on 16 January was when Joe knocked on my door and said he had been outvoted and I would be in the team. That can't have been easy for him and must have put him in a difficult predicament.

Games against Warrington are always tough and my return was no different. I played at fullback and I honestly felt like I had never been away. It was a typical league match, televised on a Saturday and no one scored any tries. The club hadn't lost a game for 20-odd matches and lo and behold I came back into the team, ousting Frankie, and we lost 6–4.

That didn't do a lot for my confidence to be honest but over the next six games I got back into form and into some sort of rhythm with the kicking too. I kicked 12 goals and scored two tries, then, in my seventh game back, we lost to Wigan 7–2 in the second round of the Challenge Cup. This turned out to be my last game for the club that season. I honestly don't remember getting hurt in that game but I read somewhere that I broke my thumb during the second half. All I know is that I didn't play particularly well and that was me for the rest of the season—but I don't remember breaking my thumb either. Roy Evans went in the corner in the last minute to give Wigan the win and I should have probably covered it.

After the match I went home to Bynea and there were rumours I had quit the club. That wasn't true, as I just wanted to spend some time at home recovering from what had happened that season. After doing some digging it seems that I was in line to play against Oldham on 13 March but Coan and the Board went with Frankie. The Board's minutes read that they suggested I play in the 'A' Team for a while to get my eye back in so to speak, but I still didn't want to do that and as a result I was not considered for the first team either.

When I was out of the team we lost a couple more games, but went on to top the League to go alongside the Lancashire League and Lancashire Cup Final wins—with Frankie Barrow at fullback. As much as the fans endeared themselves to me and my style, it was natural for them to like a home-grown local to do well. As a 'foreigner' I was more often than not going to have to prove myself. Fans looked for the good things with local players and for the bad things with non-local players. I suppose that is just human nature.

I did make one brief appearance at the very end of the season—as an unused substitute in the 15–7 Championship Final loss to Halifax. It was difficult to feel part of the club that year. Although I was buzzing in those first two games when I didn't miss a single goal, in the others I was trying just to get back to my best. I suppose I didn't feel part of that team that went so well.

Back then Saints were full of class players anyway and deserved success. John Mantle was bloody brilliant. He listened and carried out your instructions. Alex Murphy and Wilfie Smith would interchange and Peter Harvey was stand off. Joe Coan couldn't handle someone like Murph because he was his own player. Alex thought he knew best all the time and I suppose you could say he was uncoachable. But then again what could Joe teach him anyway? Joe couldn't get into players' minds; he could only get them fit.

Murphy played scrum half, stand off and centre in his time at the club and after the Challenge Cup Final in 1966 he just wanted to play scrum half. But Joe brought in Tommy Bishop the following season for £5,500 and that meant Alex sat on the sidelines for 12 months as he said he would only play on position. Did Joe want to move him on by bringing in Bishop? It's all politics perhaps.

On 27 April 1965 I put in a transfer request because of the lack of opportunities at first team level. I didn't want to play in the 'A' Team and with a Great Britain tour coming up, I needed to play regularly and, I suppose, kick regularly as well. I had more chance of going on tour as a goal kicking fullback than just a fullback.

There were regular 'A' Team players throughout the league who would never get a sniff at first team games. They still carved out a decent career a grade below. I felt I'd had a decent seven games back and done everything I could by getting fit. Okay, playing in the 'A' Team after an injury is fair enough but if you then play more games, you become classed as an 'A' Team player and I didn't want to be classed as one.

The Board listed me at £8,000 and insisted they wouldn't take anything less. It was nice to be wanted! Leeds came in for me but wanted me to head over for a trial period over at Headingley—and that was rejected out of hand. I was happy being at St Helens. It had been my home for three seasons and I felt I had established myself as a first team regular and also as a rugby league player. I just wanted to play and would have played anywhere, even forgoing my kicking duties. The kicking aspect was important if I wanted to be selected for GB. I think the Board must have thought Frankie's form was worthy of a first team place for the rest of the season.

My ambition was to go on tour and I wanted the opportunity to show all my assets to GB—I needed to catch people's eye and show off all my attributes. Therefore I wanted to kick. Frankie had put in for a transfer at that time as 'A' Team rugby wasn't for him either. He had played first team but had to play second fiddle to me when I came back. It's totally understandable from his point of view that he took this course of action.

The Board were obviously undecided. They had both of us on the list and it took them at least six months to make my transfer public and put an £8,000 fee on me. Lots of clubs were interested in me—as I said earlier Leeds wanted me to go on trial, but the St Helens' Board barred it. Workington wanted me too and they invited Jacqueline and me there one weekend to have a look at houses.

Leeds made the only concrete offer I was aware of. The Board, to their credit, reckoned I had been playing rugby league for a while and wondered why I needed to go on trial to prove I could play. Leeds wanted to look at my leg I suppose. With a tag of a broken leg plus the fee, I could understand their reluctance to come straight in with an offer.

They wanted the best of both worlds. I was disappointed at the time because I wanted to go—and, frustratingly the guy they signed, Bev Risman, went on to be capped as, you've guessed it—a goal kicking fullback!

7

'A SIGNIFICANT CHANGE THAT WOULD EFFECTIVELY CHANGE MY CAREER...'

Coming up north was a real culture shock and the pressure to show what I could do was always there. I was Saints' big money signing and a 'foreigner' so I had to prove to the fans and the rugby league community that I was the real thing.

Coming back after a bad 1964–65 season felt like I was starting over again—especially when someone with the class of Frankie Barrow wanted my spot. In fact, with Frankie being fullback the season previous, I wanted his spot. Every game was a trial and I had to be on my best form to keep my place. Two players were vying for one position and both wanted to impress the coach. It was nice to be back—and I had a good run at the beginning of that season—but something was missing. I kicked two goals against Halifax at home on 20 August, but could have hit more and to make it worse for me, Len Killeen was kicking them from all over the place too.

Eight days later in Castleford, I scored a try and kicked five goals to win a feisty match that had a load of fighting. The fans were also throwing stuff at us when we were behind the posts! We went 19 league games unbeaten to start the season and if you look at our pack, you can see why. We had Albert Halsall, Cliff Watson, Ray French, John Mantle and John Warlow; they were predominantly rugby union players and were all good, mobile players. They had tremendous engines as well as ability in abundance. Mervyn Hicks played that year too. We also had some crafty hookers in Bobby Dagnall and Bill Sayer who signed from Wigan. It was a bruising pack filled with players that could move the ball well.

Cliff was big, strong and as tough as you could get. He was a drayman for Greenalls and he told me a story once about lifting barrels. The landlord of one pub said he had a 36-gallon keg to go back to the brewery. Cliff said he lifted it on the wagon no bother. The landlord said that as the keg was virtually full he would help him out, but Cliff insisted it was on the wagon. In the end he had to prove to the landlord that he had lifted a 36-gallon keg of beer—mostly full—onto the wagon himself.

Halsall was big, mobile and although he had a beer belly, he was a tremendous forward and athlete. Sayer was ageing a bit, but he was quick and could open up gaps. Frenchie was gangly but a real workhorse and Mantle could shift too. The marshals of this impressive pack were Alex Murphy, Peter Harvey—who sometimes played on the wing—Wilfie Smith then Bob Prosser came in from Newport Rugby Union. He had been red hot in sevens and the club felt he was worth a punt.

The game had unlimited tackles back then and was very physical. It had to be physical because if a team didn't have the ball, then the players had to tackle. You'd think with that sort of game teams would keep the ball all day in the middle but there was a little more craft than you see nowadays. Wingers would score more than 40 tries a season and if the gaps were there we would go for it, even if that was from the first whistle. Once we kicked the ball we lost control so we wanted to keep hold of it and use the space. The team always felt the best place for attack was in its own 25. If you had the players and the ability then you could score from your own line. Substitutions were also few and far between so you needed to play the full 80 minutes and be fit. Coan made sure we were fit so it was down to the team's ability to see us forward.

Anyway, the most controversial signing that season was Tommy Bishop. He was the only transfer that Joe Coan was actively involved in and it was a real shock to us all, as it meant Murphy moving out to centre, and he wasn't happy with that. Was Joe trying to stamp his authority on the team to prove he was the coach and not just a fitness trainer? There were certainly a few people's noses put out at that signing.

Whilst Tommy was a cracking player, they signed him from Blackpool and no disrespect, but we did ask how many decent players came from there! But he was a St Helens lad and did his job. He came in at stand off first too with Prosser at scrum half. Vollenhoven returned after a season of injury too and that was important, as he was a class act and Killen finished top of the try and goal scoring charts in that season too. In fact, the whole Saints side didn't really have a weak link.

We had players coming in from the fringes that didn't disappoint. They learnt from the older players and were easily galvanised into the side. The 'A' Team did its job back then as we automatically got players that were ready to play. The likes of Joe Egan and Frank Ward were all good players capable of coming in and doing a job. These players had played for years in the 'A' Team.

In the first 20 games of the season, I played 19 games and

missed the BBC2 Floodlit Trophy game against Leigh on 5 October with a neck strain—coincidentally the same day as my first daughter Kay was born. Come the beginning of December, things started to tweak a little bit and I found myself sitting on the bench. During the season I made two appearances as a sub, but sat on the bench not playing a number of times as well.

Our season was shaping up to be a good one and on 2 April 1966 we played Hull KR in the Challenge Cup at Knowsley Road. It was a tight tussle with a load of needle throughout and Rovers were looking at a famous win until Murphy scored in injury time—the seventh minute of extra time allowed by referee Eric Clay. I didn't play in that game but Rovers were incensed at the amount of time allowed. Len Killen kicked the winning conversion and 15,000 fans went mad. I was behind the sticks celebrating with them. Little did we know that this last gasp win would have a massive bearing on our season!

Later in the month, on 25 April, I made the move to loose forward—a significant change that would effectively change my career forever. We were due to travel to Liverpool City and Doug Laughton had hurt his knee so I suggested that I should take his place. French and Watson were out and that meant some shuffling around in the pack. I had played outside half as a schoolboy and I felt that would stand me in good stead for it. The job of a good loose is to bind the forwards and backs and I think, considering after that game I played the majority of my career there, people were surprised that I slipped into the position so easily. It was the last game of the league season and we won 28–3 to secure the League title by a point over Wigan.

In between the Hull KR and Liverpool games, the club reached the Challenge Cup final with a 12–5 win over Dewsbury at Swinton. It was a tough clash and Mick Sullivan, who had played winger for us, was their loose forward. He always was a hard bugger to be fair and he had a cracker of a game, dominating for long periods. But as he ran out of steam, we seized our chance to win. Killeen scored two tries—an 80 yarder—and kicked three goals to win the game.

Midway through the second half, John Warlow received some rough treatment at the hands of the Dewsbury forwards and a scuffle broke out. His landlady Minnie Cotton took exception to this treatment and scaled the wall, ran on and leathered Phil Lowe with her umbrella! Warlow was her adopted son really and she dealt out some justice of her own before being escorted off by the police. I bet John felt really good seeing that and we didn't rib him in the slightest…

Although in the modern game we have league games before Challenge Cup Finals, back then the Championship semi finals would take place before the Cup Final. It meant an intensive set of fixtures before the big day out at Wembley and teams always ran the risk of being hammered physically and mentally!

Our Championship semi final was against Hull KR who were obviously keen to put the Challenge Cup third round defeat behind them. To say it was a real battle was the biggest understatement ever. I played at loose forward and to be honest it was a horrible game. I hurt my hip during the 14–6 win and Warlow was concussed after a wicked tackle.

It was a real blow for me and walking off the field, I didn't know whether I would be ready for the Cup Final. In fact, even without the injury, I didn't know if I would play or not. At the club there were six or seven forwards and I was in with a shout playing at loose. There was Sayer plus five, including myself, Halsall, Watson, French, Warlow and Mantle so you could see that Coan had a problem. Everyone was fighting for their spot and it probably spurred us all on to be honest. No one wanted to miss out at Wembley.

It caused a lot of worry for the players who expected to play at Wembley—in much the same way that Frankie Barrow coming into fullback woke me up; I woke up the rest of the forwards when I moved into the pack. They were the six; the regulars and Joe had to make a tricky decision really. Sayer and Dagnall were the hookers and were safe; the rest of the pack had to fight for their spot.

There was a lot of speculation about who would play in the week leading up to the match, but I was struggling and couldn't shake off the injury. We went to Southport to train at King George School and Stuart Hall came down to film us training. I tried to hide it, but I couldn't even jog, let alone run and I missed the final and the rest of the season. In the end I made the decision for him. Would I have been picked? I don't know. The Board's minutes show that Coan would have put me on the bench if I had been fit enough. At least that's in black and white and it makes me feel a little better to know I would have been a part of the team at Wembley.

Everyone wants to play at Wembley and the whole town got behind the club for the final against Wigan. We went to Southport on Tuesday, trained and then travelled down on Thursday to stay in the Baileys Hotel in Surrey.

History shows we beat Wigan 21–2 in front of 98,536, but I was on the outside of it all despite being a member of the squad that got the Saints there. Cup Finals are for the fans and the players who take the field. If you are a non-player—injured or not playing—then you feel out of it. It is a team occasion and it is difficult to be involved. It was the disappointment really of not knowing whether I would have been picked to play in the final and also watching the team win it. Whilst I was happy for them, it was difficult to feel completely part of the day. We never looked like losing to Wigan though.

On the Saturday night we went to the Churchill's Club and when we came out there were crowds waiting for Muhammad Ali. After the final on the Sunday we went to the Eamonn Andrews show and had a great night. Ali was a guest on the show. He asked the crowd who wanted to fight him and Tommy Bishop said he wanted a go! It was a great experience but in the back of my mind there was always the question—will I ever get to Wembley again? I just didn't know and it was the pinnacle of my career.

A week later we played Halifax in the Championship Final at Swinton and won 35–12 to complete a great haul of trophies for the Saints. I didn't watch the game, deciding to go home to Wales instead. It had been hard the previous week watching from the sidelines and I didn't want to go through that again so I travelled 'home' on the day the lads went over to Swinton to be with my family.

A season that started so well for me ended disappointingly, similar to the previous season which ended with a different injury. A simple damaged nerve in my hip put pay to a Wembley appearance just as I was getting going at loose forward. In 1965–66 I made 28 appearances, scored four tries and kicked 57 goals. I also decided to withdraw my transfer request, as it was clear I would be playing in the forwards for the following season at least.

8

'LIFE WAS PRETTY GOOD AT ST HELENS BY THEN...'

Eventually, I made a record number of appearances for St Helens but in the early days I was worried the injury curse would continue. The 1966 season was an interesting one for me as I spent a number of games on the bench and said goodbye to the fullback position that had served me well over the years.

Apart from the odd game here and there, I would never play in that spot again for Saints. I played fullback for Wales once in Salford against France, and subsequently got injured again! This time I was picked at loose with Terry Price at fullback, but he turned up late. So I was back to fullback and when Terry finally arrived, he emerged from the tunnel to see me led off with blood streaming from my head. This was after the French winger kicked deep and as I fell on the ball, he kicked me in the head, splitting it open. I had to have several stitches to close up the wound and a few weeks later it was agony. On going to hospital, I discovered one of the stitches had gone septic!

I didn't fare much better the next season and I wondered if my luck would change at all. I broke my thumb in a meaningless charity game against Swinton before the campaign even got started, then came back in at fullback, had a knock to the shoulder, sat out for a bit, then did my cartilage in a Challenge Cup tie against Salford. It was frustrating as it was becoming difficult to get established. Players get used to a spell of little niggles but these were becoming more than just bangs.

Coming back with a thumb injury is all about regaining match fitness and I did that playing for the 'A' Team on 17 September against Blackpool where we won 31–9, and I kicked eight goals. In the 'A' Team I landed 14 in total from three games before I returned on 26 September against Salford, ended up on the wing and scored. I also played scrum half against Leigh and we won 4–0. Bishop was sent off and I moved to cover his position as it was the natural thing to do for a loose forward. Killeen had kicked a goal, but was also injured so I kicked too.

I just started to make my way back—and felt very comfortable with what was happening—when my knee locked in that Salford game on 3 February 1967. A small piece of cartilage snapped off and went right behind the back, which meant I couldn't straighten my knee. It was permanently half bent and it meant an operation and ended my season. Doctor Herron, who was the specialist at Everton, did the surgery and within two days assessed and fixed my knee. I was in bed for a couple of days then on crutches for a few weeks.

It was a strange old season for the team and me. We never seemed to get anywhere near the sort of form that gave us an impressive haul of trophies in 1966. It didn't help that Alex Murphy refused to play for the side either. In fact, when I broke my finger in that 27–13 defeat to Swinton, Cliff Watson, Tommy Bishop, Murphy, French, Mantle and Killeen were all out because of one reason or another. When Bishop came in Murphy moved into the three quarters and we won four cups. At the beginning of the following season Murphy decided he wouldn't turn out for the Saints at centre. That was a real shock to the team.

It transpired that Coan had been to the Board and insisted that Murphy played at centre and they agreed. Coan thought this was best for the team because Alex was a more versatile player than Bishop, who had been signed from Blackpool as a scrum half. I suppose Murphy knew when Bishop came his days at scrum half were numbered. He tackled Harry Cook about this because he felt his strength was at half back and he was out of it at centre. Murphy refused to play as a protest and eventually moved to Leigh as player-coach the following year. It was his choice to stop playing; his teammates certainly didn't want him to stop and missed his skills.

We struggled at points that year, yet we had a quality player in the stands and he could have made a difference. I'm not sure if he was told to play at centre otherwise he wouldn't play or if he had the attitude of if I don't play scrum half I am not playing. Peter Harvey was a stand off and he sometimes had to play on the wing. Murphy was a local lad and quite rightly proud of it. He had certainly made good and achieved everything in the game from a very early age. He was never happy when new players were signed and got more money than him and would really stir things up.

At the end of the season Len Killeen also left the club to join Balmain, which was another unexpected departure. He seemed settled at the Saints but must have had an offer that was too good to refuse: they came in for him and he went. Len scored spectacular tries and kicked superb goals. He had a free and easy attitude to life and the hard tops [pitches] over there would have suited him. He wasn't a physical player—and in England the game was very physical back then.

The following season the four tackle rule was introduced. With unlimited tackles, a team could hold onto the ball all day and grind the opposition down. Packs could establish themselves and create physical games. When we won four trophies in 1966, the side had an abundance of ability, strength, mobility, skill and speed and were capable of playing football. That pack could keep going all day and utilise the gaps to work their way up the field, and then pile on the points. Teams could keep the ball for as long as they wanted and the opposition could only get it back by winning it or if a team lost it. If the pack was fit, like ours, capable of recycling the ball and keeping it going for a long time, they could stifle the game. Saints also had the guile to get it wide when needed and unlock the defence.

When the game was limited to four tackles, it was a culture shock throughout the league. Saints, in particular, struggled in that first season. Our 1966 team could control the game, tackle all day and have the class and vision to play rugby. We could soak up the pressure and then use it. Four tackles made things a little manic. It was a potential danger to lose the ball early, so we would sometimes kick it on the first tackle to surprise our opponents. I always thought it made the game a little frantic and hit and miss.

Our team was set up for unlimited tackles as we could starve the opposition of the ball and get them to use all their strength to tackle us. Tackling was much more of an art back then. Our forwards could get two or three players to tackle them and then we had the class to use the gaps out wide as a result. Nowadays, you get five players in a tackle and you can't say they get back into position straightaway...that is where the vision has gone out of the modern game. These days, teams don't use the gaps as much as they should.

In the seventies there was also talk of reducing the game to 12 or 11 men a side. That was tipping the nod to the coaches who liked seven a side. If they had reduced to, say, 10 a side, athlete Dwain Chambers would have been happy! In my day, especially in that 1966 team, we brought people into the middle to tackle us and then pushed the ball wide. In fact, all the teams I played in had players capable of that—the Chisnalls, Mantles, Nichols, Warlows and Halsalls all knew what to do and got it wide. Halsall got three tries in Championship final by going out wide.

I think the authorities were concerned that Saints, in particular, could keep hold of the ball for most of the game if they wanted. In 1966, Alex Murphy went offside all the time because it gave a penalty to the opposition. They would kick it into touch and then try to win it from the scrum. But Sayer and co were too good in the pack to lose the ball at the scrum. Now, you can't blame Murphy for doing that can you? Teams will always adapt to the rules and play them to their own advantage.

I understand why they limited the number of tackles though. It quickened up the game and showed that the real art of rugby league—what set it apart from union—was the tackling. It was the art of stopping the opposition scoring. But four tackles almost took the game to touch rugby because rugby league needs tackles.

Therefore, the 1967–68 season was one of change, and four games in, Widnes snapped up Ray French. We didn't know much about the deal, but it turned out Ray's last game was a 13–11 win at home to Wakefield on 28 August. Next thing, Frank Myler was on the team sheet four days later at Barrow. Ray says he was up a ladder painting his house when his wife ran out saying there was a call from the Saints' Chairman who wanted him to go to Widnes. Apparently, Ray told his wife a few times he couldn't go because he was up a ladder—he'd be able to go later. I don't think he realised that Harry wanted him to go permanently! Saints also brought in Bob Wanbon, Graham Rees—a second rower—Mike McNeil and John Walsh at various points during the year. Voll left the club to go home.

We also had a lot of youngsters coming through that season too. Joe Egan, Eric Chisnall, Tony Barrow, John Houghton, Peter Gartland and Tony Karalius all got a taste of the action and Bob Blackwood and Peter Douglas came through from the 'A' Team too. By far and away the biggest change was the resignation of Joe Coan in January 1967. He left because he couldn't get the team to adapt—particularly to the new four tackle rule. A lot of lucky players and coaches in this game have gained medals when perhaps they shouldn't have.

Before he was the gaffer, Joe was on the payroll as a keep fit man. He wanted the accolades, got the team fit—doing his job of course—but I think he wanted to take the plaudits and be good enough to be first man. I don't think he was up to it. Would we have won the trophies without him? Perhaps we wouldn't have been as fit, but the ability was always in the team. He wanted his team to play in a certain way rather than the pack just grinding teams down—we couldn't do that with the four tackle rule anyway. He hadn't brought the flair in and at this point the team needed it as we had the ability and talent to score from all over, but we didn't utilise or realise our full potential.

When Cliff Evans came in from Swinton, we were excited. He coached Swinton during their glory days in the early sixties and they were a good team with some flair. We expected this flair to come to us too and he was instrumental in bringing in some good signings like Wanbon. He was also keen to play me at loose forward—although I had a good spell at fullback that season with Graham Rees at loose forward—and continue with the kicking duties. Rees was brought in as a running second rower to get us to Wembley, but he didn't get there for the next couple of years!

All in all I played 39 games and scored 180 points. I wanted to kick goals, as I wanted to tour with GB, but playing loose forward and not kicking, didn't really matter. The team had to come first. Throughout that season I missed a few games because of minor facial and rib injuries but the knee seemed fine. My transfer request was history as well and I have to say life was good at St Helens by then!

Injuries had kept away and things were going really well for me. I made a good comeback in the end. I came to Saints in 1962, got married in 1964 and had a child in 1966. Despite having a bad run with injuries, things were going well and I had no regrets. To be honest with you, my injuries coincided with me getting married but the wife won't like me saying that! I broke my leg two weeks before I got married and some said it was an easy way of getting out of it! Before the injuries came, I was a carefree young lad who was playing and having fun. It could have been a hard time after I was injured but getting married not only helped me to settle at the club but it also meant I had support whilst injured.

Jacqueline stuck by me during those dark days and it was good to go home to a supportive wife. Being married kept me going really. Without her support, I could have taken my ball home. It helped me to grow up and she made me realise that with hard work and perseverance I could stick around and have a good career. She also stuck by me when I had hundreds of promotions to do in the late sixties and seventies. I had to take the cup round to schools and social clubs, and I appeared in the local papers each week holding up Beauty Queens and such. It was a hard life.

In 1967–68, we took some big scalps before Evans came in but that was down to the ability of the team and the sheer bloody mindedness of the players not to give up. On 15 September, Alex Murphy brought his Leigh team to Knowsley Road and we battered them 22–0 in front of more than 20,000 fans. He always thought he was the only player in the Saints team and without him we wouldn't play as well, but we did. He let the team down being club captain and refusing to play and it was clear we all wanted to put one over him. He would have wanted to beat us too! It was nice for us to win though.

At the beginning of October we drew two-a-piece against Warrington in the Lancashire Cup Final—in a pretty appalling game all round—but won 13–10 two months later in the replay. Perhaps the games were too far apart as only around 7,000 turned up to watch the second game.

Vollenhoven was captain that day and John Mantle ended up pushed out onto the wing at various points in the game. Mantle was not as quick as Voll—he had played centre—but was quick for a packman. The adage that you can't put forwards into backs but you can put backs into forwards might be true in that case!

The game was nip and tuck all the way and I missed a couple of kicks so for the best of the team, we gave the duties John Houghton who promptly banged over a couple. Eric Chisnall scored as did John Warlow and Les Jones and we gave Voll a trophy in his last year at the club. We knew he was going back home and to grab him a trophy at the first time of asking that season was extra special.

Voll left the club as a total legend and probably the greatest ever winger in the history of the game. The esteem he is held in when he comes back to the town underlines the impact the man had on St Helens. He finished with something like 390 tries in 400 appearances but it wasn't just his try-scoring exploits that made him a great player. He always said a lot in the dressing room to get the team going and had this thing about getting his feet and particularly his balls right. He put cotton wool around his toes in his boots and smeared Vaseline around his balls so he would be comfortable. It obviously worked too.

Voll also came across and tackled rather than just stay out on the wing. He was a hard worker and would play in the centre if asked. It was not his favoured position but he would do whatever was asked of him. One thing I liked about him was that he would always make his mind up early on when he was one-on-one with the opposition. He was so quick; he would go in and go out, and they couldn't catch him.

He was strong too—he would hand off and use his body strength and the other player's strength to push himself away. He was also an Olympic sprinter and a South African rugby union international. He would score off his own line, from any part of the field and would always back himself. After the game we put him on our shoulders and then carried him from the bar afterwards. We had a few at the club's bar as well as a good sing.

Whilst we're talking about try scoring exploits let's not forget my hat trick against Halifax that season too! It was superb! I remember it well. It was 19 August 1968, Championship round one at Knowsley Road. We won 31–2 and I kicked five goals. They were a decent side as well. I basically backed up, followed Bishop and popped up for three tries. They weren't 100 yarders...just 99ers ...

I always backed myself to score when I followed Tommy. I learnt from an early age always to follow the scrum half when they are close to the line. Incidentally, Tommy was a test player and I suppose they could have looked at him and brought me into the GB set up too as we linked up well. Ah well!

9

'I LIKED THE OCCASIONAL BEER...'

It can be frustrating being in and out of the team, especially when you know that it is predominately because of injury rather than poor form. Being dropped because of poor performance is easier to fix; you work hard in training and in reserve games and then hopefully impress enough to get your chance again.

I know what it is like to sit out for large chunks of a season only to come back, and get injured again. As I said earlier, I still make a point of speaking to, and involving, the injured players at Saints to make sure they aren't forgotten and feel part of the club.

So in 1968–69, I was glad not only to get a good run of games, but also to play most of the season and perform at a level that was probably expected of me. I played 46 games that season—and one at sub—and scored 317 points. These days, players will hit around 250 in 30 games, but of course there are more points for a try these days. What I'm actually saying is that I am happy with that return! I cannot imagine any modern day player wanting to play in so many games! But the knee felt good, the knocks weren't coming and I felt good. I was married, living in a nice town and things couldn't be better.

I had a lot of time for Cliff Evans and one of his first tasks that season was to replace the irreplaceable Tom Van Vollenhoven. No one could have replaced Voll's style, scoring prowess, ability and dry wit so when Frank Wilson came in from Cardiff Rugby Union he was on a hiding to nothing. He'd played for Western Wales against New Zealand and he did all right.

The press made a big thing of it because he was, as they called him, 'coloured'. It's tough to imagine in this day and age why it was a big thing, but back then it was. Frank was confident in his abilities and was probably the first coloured player to play for East Wales, so he was buzzing when he came up. And he did well—scoring a try against Whitehaven on his debut. He scored tries that others may not have scored and had blistering pace. Like Voll he would come in to tackle from the wing and do his bit.

He played in the 1972 Challenge Cup Final but was left out for the 1976 final against Widnes. Eric Ashton used to ask the senior players and captains for their opinions before a big game. We had a chat to decide if Frank was fit or not because he had a hamstring problem. A few said he was fit and I didn't think he was and said he shouldn't play…and he didn't. Wembley isn't the place to test fitness and it was a big risk to play someone who wasn't 100 per cent fit.

Telling a player who has appeared in most of the games in a particular season that they won't be in the Cup Final line up can't be easy for a coach. But, on the flip side, asking someone to do a job in a final when they aren't fit puts loads of pressure on their teammates. In the end, Peter Glynn came off the bench and scored two tries.

Like me and a few others in the team, Frank came up north and did well. But, like me, he also had to prove himself constantly as he was also classed as a foreigner. As outsiders, we didn't know what we were coming to, and it was a bonus if people accepted us for what we were and what we did. Frank repaid them with a ton of tries.

Frank was one of only a few players to come in that season and the team, as a whole, was very settled. There was a little swapping and changing in the pack, but nothing disrupted the flow of the team. I was settled in my loose forward position and perhaps all of us playing together regularly was the start of something big at the club. We seemed to all kick on that season and, with Cliff Evans, play even better as a team. We showed that by beating Wakefield away in the first game of the season 5–0 with Tommy Bishop as captain and doing the double over them a few weeks later at Knowsley Road. In fact all through the season we were there or thereabouts for winning trophies.

We cruised into the final of the Lancashire Cup beating Wigan, Widnes and Leigh along the way to face an Oldham team that, in all fairness, we were expected to beat. But in front of a decent crowd at Wigan on 25 October we found ourselves 2–0 down at half time. Oldham were a good team in the fifties and sixties and it was a cup tie, but it was a bit of a shock as such to be down at half time. Cliff wasn't a blaspheming man at all, but he may well have changed his mind in that half time break! He certainly gave it to us!

Geoff Fletcher played for Oldham and ran us off the park in the first half. But we knuckled down and scored 30 unanswered points in the second half to win the trophy again. Once we were 10 points clear of Oldham, they crumbled and we ran away with it. Realistically, even back then only Saints, Leeds and Wigan could come back from that far down.

A few weeks later we found ourselves in the BBC2 Floodlit Trophy final at Wigan. The competition caught the imagination of both the fans and players. Being live on TV was a big thing back then. All the players wanted to play in that competition especially as Saints were on TV. As I'd signed from Wales, appearing on TV for St Helens let people in Wales know (whether they supported or criticised me) that I had not disappeared into the sunlight and reminded them I was still playing well.

And in the end, that can only be a boost. I wanted to be a part of rugby all the time, especially as part of a successful team. Appearing on TV was classed as being successful at the time, and Saints played on TV quite a bit, especially when games were also televised on a Saturday afternoon. Kids grew up watching players lift the cup on TV and they wanted to emulate their heroes. For us, even at our tender age, that was what we wanted to do—get on and perform well on TV. It's all about childhood dreams I suppose. The BBC2 Floodlit Trophy caught the imagination and there is still talk of it today.

We lost the game! We were winning 4–2 with five minutes to go and had the ball in our hands. Instead of going the full four tackles and playing out the set, Cliff Watson, a great player who never shirked his workload, just turned around and threw the ball out. I suppose everyone expected him to take the ball forward as we were in our own 25, but perhaps he saw something on elsewhere. You can't blame him for that at all. But the ball just went to ground and Cliff Hill, Wigan's stand off, picked it up and scooted under the sticks. We lost 7–4. We lost the game because of our own mistake and we were gutted, but that's the way it goes sometimes. That game sticks in the mind as it seemed that every time I went to Wigan to play in a cup tie of some sort we lost.

Cliff Watson left the club in March 1970 to join Tommy Bishop in Australia. As a result, Evans made me captain—a surprise as the conversation we had about it was so formal I thought I had been dropped. These players left big holes to fill in the team, but we won the league the season afterwards so I suppose we coped. Cliff and Tommy were very popular in the town. Cliff was a good player; he came to the club on trial and proved to be one of the best in the game and the supporters loved that. Both he and Tommy were workhorses that never shirked anything. They were both prepared to listen and would carry out instructions without thinking.

They had a nice payday in Oz and who could blame them for going? Initially, Tommy and Cliff's situation in Australia was similar to my situation when I first came to Saints from Wales as they also faced a lot opposition from fans and players. Rather like with me, players and fans looked at their mistakes, rather than at the positives in their games. Fortunately they proved themselves by winning trophies over there in their first season.

Although Tommy left at the end of the year to join Cronulla, he did get injured that season and his brother, Alan Bishop took over for a couple of games. Alan was a bit of a flyer and wasn't as physical as Tommy. That isn't a criticism, though, as he was a good player. Whilst Tommy was a competitive and physical player, Alan was more of a Bob Prosser character; he would float about and throw the most amazing passes around. He could get the ball away from the ruck in a flash.

Alan settled in well when he came into the team, but the following season Geoff Heaton came back and it was harder for Alan to get a sniff. Geoff played in the 62–63 Lancashire Cup final before going to Liverpool Stanley, but then we signed him back as he was always a good player. As Alan found out, there's always someone who keeps popping up to take your place. I found that out when I was injured. New players come in and you have to work hard to get back in the team.

At the time, St Helens was run by Beechams, Pilkingtons and

Saints. The town had some great social clubs back then and the club was part of the social scene of the time. The public bar on match day, now at the club, used to be a real hive of activity and everyone loved going there. I was assistant steward of the club before 1964 and Charlie Matthews was the first steward there even though he had no idea whatsoever about how to run a bar. He was an ex Pilks driver, in his late sixties.

I had pulled a pint at my aunt's bar in Wales when there were no tills and the money went in the tin. And, I'd had a few pints in my time so I was ideally placed to become the club's barman! Anyway, 'Touchlines' as such, was a social club right up until the end of the sixties then it transformed into a nightclub. The Supporters Club, who ran it, handed the Rugby League Club £6,000; that's how much they were making as a social club. When it became a nightclub with a 2 p.m. licence, it died a death and has struggled ever since. The Board, to their folly, leased the restaurant and gave away its responsibility.

Because the town was thriving with industry, clubs like Parr Conservative and Hardshaw were probably more popular than pubs back then. They attracted stars and the likes of Kathy Kirby and Bob Monkhouse appeared at the social club at Saints.

Team spirit was good in those days. We were all in our early twenties and courting and we stayed behind after a game together. We all got to know each other without getting too close. No one was left out. Those social events and togetherness got us through some tough times. It spilt over into the supporters too; we all mixed together which went down well with the supporters. We'd unwind and then be ready for work on Monday.

I also became a dad for the second time in 1968 when Suzanne was born—with my third, Sian born in 1971. Families can be troublesome sometimes and after a few beers, very confusing. One time, when we lived in Rainhill, my wife's, auntie's daughter Carol came to babysit. She stayed over in the 'best' room (ours), as we liked to show her how thankful we were. As I have stated, I have always loved a beer. After a biggish night out, I got up to go to the toilet and got back into my own bed. I then put my arm round her and fell asleep. She woke up wondering who this strange bloke in her bed was, got up and climbed into bed with the wife, waking her up to tell her what happened. The wife got out of bed with her and came into bed with me. Of course, I got daggers in the morning and had to explain my actions. As every good man should do, I faced the music bravely. Of course, I couldn't remember what had happened.

My life and misfortunes with beer continued when I became a drayman. It was a great job. I was fit, lifting barrels, having a pint and this was as good as any weight training. I was in my pomp, shifting stuff, it was great. I might not have had bulging muscles as if I was lifting weights, but I needed balance to lug barrels around. You have to throw them up and then drop them down and it was great fun. I eventually left that job to have my own tipper wagon—I was trying to do better!

That was fun, and sometimes interesting, too. I stopped the wagon once on the way to a game as I saw a house on fire in Haydock. I went in the house to find an old woman trying to put out the fire downstairs. Her husband was upstairs so I ran up and got him out. When I came down, she had put out the fire, told me it was fine and wished me well! I jumped on the wagon and went to play a game.

I was always working, training, out touring with trophies and such and my wife would tell me she brought the kids up on her own. I went training directly from work and the kids were asleep by the time I got back. Jacqueline took the kids to Wales now and again and I would come back and work. It was hard not seeing the little ones growing up, but I was providing for them and that was important. I was providing for my family just like my dad did for Keri and me. It was a great occasion when we went to Wembley as Jacqueline could come to the game. I may come across as a family man these days, but it was very difficult back then to try to find a balance.

It didn't help family life when I played for Wales—but Jacqueline was well used to it and it was always an honour to play for my country. In November 1968, we played at Salford and lost 24–17 to England, and then we travelled to Paris in March 1969 to lose 17–13 to France. Again, like playing in the BBC2 Floodlit Trophy, playing for Wales was a good opportunity to show the people back home that you could still play a bit and hadn't failed. I had been at Knowsley Road for seven years so I didn't want the people in Wales to forget that I was doing well for myself.

Normally we would have played in Toulouse or Narbonne, so to play in Paris was a big thing. And despite us losing, we played well. The Welsh problem wasn't the number of players we had, it was more that we struggled to find players of more specialised positions like hooker or scrum half. We had plenty of forwards but played lads out of position to fill gaps. That could get a team through the odd club game, but at international level you need players in their own positions.

It was a great occasion. To be playing with John Warlow, Gordon Lewis and the rest was brilliant and we had a good time too. Post match was superb as we had a massive banquet and lots of wine. We liked the occasional beer (cough) but the French gave us wine all the time. We couldn't cope with that!

I can still see Terry Price, who died a young man, standing on a seat leading the choir and everyone joining in. I also remember Warlow turning green and disappearing outside to be sick. He thought he had found a quiet place, but everyone could see him through the window puking for Wales!

They were great times and it's a shame the Welsh team didn't play more often. We tried to keep it going and went to the World Cup, but we needed to take more risks and play a few more games. They were always big occasions and I loved playing in them. The fans came out to support us too.

They reminded me of the big derbies that we played in—all eyes were on you and you wanted to put one over the opposition. And if you did something special people would talk about it for ages. I kicked 10 goals against Wigan on Boxing Day in 1969 and I ask you, how many people have kicked 10 goals against Wigan in one game? We won 53–11. It was the prelude to a great season that brought a Championship trophy.

In 1969–70, Cliff Evans had a very settled team that was capable of scoring a lot of tries and defending well. John Walsh could score and kick, Frank Wilson ended up with 30 odd tries and Les Jones close to 40 tries. We scored more points than anyone in the league and conceded the least. Unbelievably we still finished third!

Walsh and young Billy Benyon were the centres—Albert Halsall was still in the pack. Alan Whittle was half back and he was what you could describe as a livewire. He was certainly a stop start player—a real jinker who would catch players out very easily with his moves. They couldn't pinpoint him. Frank Myler was strong and fluid and he linked with Heaton really well. It was a decent side.

Cliff Evans had a tremendous rugby brain, not far behind that of Eric Ashton. I would put them both in the category of top coaches. The only difference was that one had been a top player and the other hadn't. Also Cliff was affected by asthma and he used to get out of breath. Whether that caused him some trouble or not, I don't know. Cliff's method was to keep things simple and devise some planned moves.

In one game, Bill Sayer scored from a criss-cross move that Evans had planned and worked out on the training field. The idea was Sayer passed to me, then ran around, John Mantle came on to it like a train, popped it up for Sayer and scored under the sticks. Back in those days we did loads of run-arounds and it caught teams unaware. Sometimes though, we didn't need fancy moves to win and we ground down the opposition through sheer pace and physical play in our pack. But for some reason our side failed to win the silverware it deserved that season. We consistently played well all year, but didn't top the league when perhaps we should have done and missed out on the Challenge Cup Final when we lost 6–3 to Castleford in the semi final.

Castleford kicked three drop goals, whilst Les Jones scored our solitary points—the first try they conceded in the cup. The 'droppers' on that day were Mal Reilly, Alan Hardisty and Bill Kirkbride. Kirk-bloody-bride! He had never kicked a goal before. Jones scored his try early on and I hit the post on the conversion from the touchline. The semi is a game so near and, if you lose a game, so far. Losing semi finalists are never mentioned but if you lose in a final, at least you were there to enjoy the occasions so to speak.

Castleford are very much like St Helens and, like the Saints, are historically good at producing youngsters. Alan Hardisty was cracker and a little underrated. He certainly didn't get the plaudits he deserved, and still doesn't. Keith Hepworth was a hard bugger, a busy bee and they fed off each other. Alan had a canny knack of being a ghost as such. He scored a lot of tries through interceptions, appearing out of nowhere and could set things up at the drop of a hat.

We were bound to face each other again that season and on 2 May 1970, we travelled over to Cas to play the Championship semi final. Again, it was another tight affair and we drew 9–9.

Wearing my cap for Wales in the Coleshill line up

The Bynea team that won the Camarthen sevens. My dad is on the right on the back row

The Dewar Shield winning team

The Llanelli team, 1959–60

The Aberavon team that took home the Welsh Championship in 1960–61

Practice match 1962-63—possibly my first appearance at Knowsley Road. The First Team always used to play the 'A' Team in a pre season match. I'm on the far right and Len Killeen is about to come onto the ball. The player on the far left is Jackie Pimblett, who later played for Recs and died when a scrum collapsed on him

Stan McCormack teaching me the 'play the ball' after my signing in 1962

Away it goes—one of many during my early league days as a fullback
© *St Helens Reporter*

I made my debut for Saints with Len Killeen (bottom right) against Leigh in the Western Division Championship in 1962–63. We won 21–3, and I kicked six goals. Saints team, back row: Fred Leyland, Ray French, Bob Dagnall, John Tembey, Cliff Watson, Kel Coslett, Keith Northey. Front row: Tom van Vollenhoven, John Donovan, Bill Major (capt), Alan Briers, Wilf Smith, Len Killeen. © *St Helens Reporter*

First game back on 16 January 1965 v Warrington at Wilderspool after breaking my leg. We lost 4–6 on goal kicks!

1967 Lancashire Cup Final team: the victorious Saints hold aloft Vol after beating Warrington in a replay 13–10 © St Helens Reporter

Winning the Lancashire Cup again in 1968—after beating Oldham 30–2
© *St Helens Reporter*

1970 Challenge Cup semi final, Saints v Castleford at Swinton. We lost 6–3 and I missed two chances in the second half. There was a strong wind!

1970 Championship Final, battered and bruised, we celebrated the 24–12 win over Leeds

1971–72 Wembley toss—a traditional pre match ritual. I wait for Leeds captain Alan Hardisty to toss the coin before kick off at Wembley in 1972, with referee Eric Lawrinson and his two touch judges looking on

© St Helens Reporter

1971 Championship Final: before the game with a proud Geoff Pimblett

1971 Championship Final, holding aloft the trophy after beating Wigan, 16–12

*1971 Championship
Final post match: we'd
had a few at this point*

*1971 Championship
Final post match…and
we'd had a few more by
the time we hit town!*

*European Champions!
Lifting up another
trophy after beating
French side St Gaudens
92–11 on aggregate*

Wember-glee—leading the team out for the big one

Championship Trophy 1975 cup presentation © St Helens Reporter

1975 Wales v France. The first rugby league match at Swansea for 24 years! A crowd of more than 20,000 saw Wales beat France 21–8. I kicked four goals
© South Wales Evening Post

Crooners all! Recording a couple of songs at the Magnum Studios in Hyde for the World Cup. The nominated singers were Jim Mills, Les Pearce, Ron Simpson, Colin Dixon, Tony Fisher and me

Tackling Alex Murphey – always had him in my pocket

1975 World Cup saoking up the sun with some Welsh colleagues over in Australia and New Zealand

Scoring one of my rare tries—this time against Warrington in the 1972 Challenge Cup semi final replay. Great technique!

Travelling in style—the 1976 Challenge Cup Final coach

Receiving the 1975–76 Challenge Cup from the Rt Hon. Margaret Thatcher, Leader of the Opposition

Wembley 1976 Challenge Cup Final: cup winners again!
© *County Press News and Picture Agency*

1976 Challenge Cup Final Celebrations— our return home from Wembley
© *St Helens Reporter*

Smashing Salford's John Butler in the 1976 Premiership Final at Swinton

1976 Premiership Final: winners again!

Past players Huddersfield 1995. A selection of Saints' past players join the game's centenary celebrations at the George Hotel, Huddersfield. Back row: John Mantle, Mick Murphy, Alex Murphy, Ray French, Peter Harvey, George Nicholls, Kel Coslett. Front row: Geoff Pimblett, Austin Rhodes, Glyn Moses, Alan Prescott, Bob Dagnall, Duggie Greenall

Sailing away on the QEII as part of the Liverpool team to win a national Whitbread contest for selling the most Heineken

All smiles: my family have stuck with me through thick and thin

A proud moment as I was named Honorary Life President of the club in 2008. Eamonn McManus gave a speech to the crowd on presenting me with the honour and mentioned I had 'relegated' Wigan. It got the loudest cheer of the night but I wasn't impressed
© St Helens RLFC

My family then...   *...and now*

The replay on 4 May wasn't kind to Castleford as they were due to play Wigan in the Challenge Cup a few days later. With that in mind, they played virtually a full strength reserve team. Not that it made any difference, as at one point they were 12–10 up. But Frank Wilson picked up a ball on his own 20 and scorched 80 yards to the pavilion end and we knew from there we weren't going to lose.

Frank ended up with a hat trick in our 21–10 win over there and then was promptly dropped for the final against Leeds as he had made a mistake in the first half! Wilson missed two games all season and one of those was the final! Evans could be ruthless!

Before the game, Cliff decided to resign from the club and that made it more important for us to send him out on a high. Travelling from Greater Manchester was too much, so he eventually ended up at Salford. In my opinion Cliff was one of the best coaches I played under, although I may say that because he gave me the captaincy. He had a tremendous footballing brain with some great set moves.

The final was at Odsal, which wasn't the best of places to go when the weather was rough. On this occasion, it began sunny, went gloomy and deteriorated. It rained, hailed and became darker as the game went on. It was also very cold. Cliff decided to play young Eric Prescott in Wilson's place against Alan Smith who was world class, and we were all concerned about how he would get on. We trusted Cliff, of course, but Smith had pace to burn. And when he skinned Prescott in the first seven minutes, you could say we were right.

Whether that was the wakeup call Prescott needed, I don't know. Prescott was outstanding from that point on and didn't give Smith a sniff. He ended up scoring two tries. And we needed them as at one point, when up 5–3, I dropped the ball out from under the sticks to the half way line—a yard from touch—and Ron Cowan caught it and scored from exactly the same spot I had just kicked. But Walsh's massive drop goal and his try alongside Prescott's tries saw us home.

Saints had threatened to win the league on a number of occasions so finally to do it was a great experience. We had a settled side back then and that made the difference. Saints were always in the mix and in order for teams to win a trophy, they had to beat a good Saints side. So finally we lifted up the trophy and had a few beers afterwards!

10

'I WAS IN MY THIRD POMP...'

I rated Cliff Evans as one of the better coaches I have played under, if not the best, alongside the late Eric Ashton MBE. But whilst Jim Challinor brought success to the club throughout the four years he was here, I didn't rate him much. He died a young man and had success as Saints and GB coach, but I can't say we got on well.

I was captain towards the end of 1969–70 and one of the first things he did was to take that honour away from me. He said he didn't like a forward being a captain and I thought he should have at the least given me a couple of games to see how I performed. He decided to give the captaincy to Billy Benyon without really knowing if he was good enough to do it.

That told me Jim wasn't a great people's person and later in my time at Saints he proved it to me. I remember John Mantle asking me on the way up to Barrow whether he was playing or not as Jim hadn't named the team. He had been at the club eight years and didn't know if he was playing! That's not right really. Then in 1974 when Jim was GB coach, he ran alongside me at training and said I had missed out of going on tour by one vote and he was really sorry. I could tell he didn't mean it. The way he approached the game didn't suit me at all.

I know he had a good playing credibility, playing successfully for Warrington, Barrow and GB. He also coached Barrow and Liverpool Stanley. Afterwards he joined GB with his mate Reg Packer. Reg wasn't a mate of mine either! I was let down by both of them a few times.

Anyway, I don't know what I did to him to be honest, but whatever existed at the club before he came; he only seemed interested in changing it. He took the captaincy off me without knowing what sort of captain I was. He gave the captaincy to Billy Benyon, but Billy, who always gave his all, lost his head on the field and Challinor had to reverse the decision and give it back to me. That can't have been easy for him. It sounds awful I know, but he hardly helped me at all, in fact I helped him, as I had to do half time talks and such during matches. For me, his contribution to the team in 1972 was nothing. It's not bitterness; I thought he treated me poorly.

When he was GB coach in 1974 with Reg Parker, I lost any remaining respect I had for them. They said they tried their best to get me in that side, but I knew that was rubbish. I knew it was hard to get into any national side, but I thought I could have a game and not let any side down. I know they had Mal Reilly, Georgie Nichols and Dougie Laughton so I just had to keep plodding on. They chose international teams in those days by committee, with all clubs represented. It was a case of 'I'll vote for your player if you vote for mine' and it was a diabolical system.

I know we had a good season that year, but we won the league the year before without him. In the end, you still have the players and we always have had someone who can do it right. Jim wasn't all bad though; he kept hold of Eddie Cheetham. He was our keep fit trainer, an absolute fanatic and had that aura of professionalism around him.

At 28 years of age I was in my third pomp. I was playing,

happy and never thought about the future. I was in my prime. I had played rugby from school age so that was all I knew. When I look at the pictures of me back then, I can't believe how fit I looked. I was lucky enough to have a good engine that could keep on going. All I wanted to do was play—that's why I'd come north—and I wasn't interested in sitting out games for a rest. I didn't mind training either and matches helped get me fit as well.

One of the things I changed over the seasons was how I kicked for goal. I used to kick the point in the same way that my hero Terry Davies did. But when I broke my leg, I noticed that I was no longer as accurate at kicking. It is difficult coming back from that sort of injury. I started off with a loose limp, then I got my running power back and finally my kicking returned. I started to put the ball upright so there was more of an area on it to kick. I went two yards back, took my time and then banged it. Getting more consistent was the key and as time went on the power and accuracy came back. I tried one of those American kicking tees as well and that didn't really work, as I couldn't set up the ball in the way I wanted to.

Whatever I did must have helped as during that season, on 19 October 1970, I booted 12 from 12 in a 42–0 win over Bradford. I allegedly scored a try that day too but I can't remember it. It was pissing with rain and I was slotting them from all over the place. I kicked some off the half way line—they were perfect conditions for me—and I kept the night going for the fans! Alex Service produced a diagram in *The March of the Saints—St Helens Rugby League Club 1945–1985* (see diagram) showing my kicks but if you examine it, it is the wrong way round.

Brian Butler played for Bradford that night and he hit Eric Prescott so hard that the lad did three summersaults, although it wasn't the hardest punch I had ever seen thrown! I went into

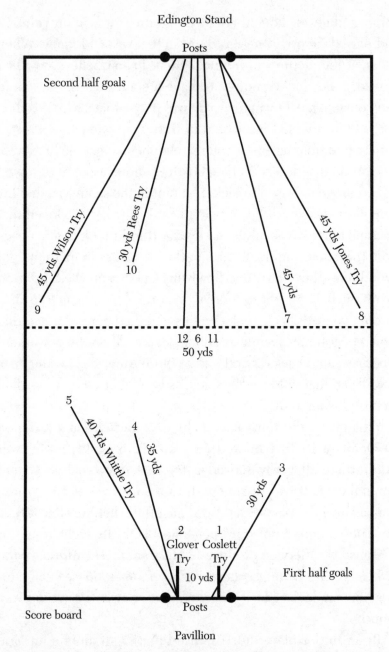

Edington Stand

Posts

Second half goals

45 yds Wilson Try

30 yds Rees Try

10

9

45 yds Jones Try

45 yds

7

8

12 6 11
50 yds

5

40 Yds Whittle Try

4

35 yds

3

30 yds

2
Glover
Try

1
Coslett
Try

10 yds

First half goals

Score board

Posts

Pavillion

My 12 from 12 kicks against Bradford on 19 October 1970, but it's not quite right!

the second row a season later in place of Eric and he played a couple at loose. He liked it so much that he asked the coach if he could play there for the rest of the season. I told Jim to tell him to bugger off, as it was my position!

I also tried wearing a skullcap but didn't like it after a while. I wore it in a couple of games and it never sat right on my head. It wasn't hiding a dodgy or wild seventies haircut either. Actually, I remember saying to our physio once that my hair was getting in my eyes and that he should cut it—during the game. He rushed me to the sidelines to give me a short back and sides—although in fact it was a good straight fringe cut.

During that season I went into business with Frankie Barrow and Basil Lowe with our own tipper wagon. We were subcontracting on the new M58 from Liverpool to the M6 with Joe Pickavance and our firm was called CBL Haulage. The business didn't last long as I don't suppose I am cut out to be a businessman. Frank and Basil left the business and I carried on, unfortunately I also inherited all the debts. For a while I worked at Fibreglass clearing the waste. It helped me pay off all the debts and gave me a nice living. But the job ended and I needed an MOT on the wagon, tax and tyres and I wondered if it was worth it. Things were tight when I worked on the motorways and it was expensive in terms of breakdowns.

In the end I was offered a job as a rep with Kerr's Minerals and, after chatting to the wife, I took it. I would have had to go back into debt to get the wagon sorted out and I didn't want mortgages and bank loans. Back then being in debt would have been wrong. Just when I thought I had cleared all the debts, a few months later I received a whopping great tax bill. So I went off to the tax office, said I couldn't afford it, and I ended up paying weekly instalments for months.

I used to park the tipper wagon on the land next to the main stand at Knowsley Road. One Sunday afternoon—we had played on the Saturday—we were down in the sponsor's car park changing a gearbox without a jack. Frank was a fitter and he said we would drop the gearbox and I had to lift the other one into place. I was on my back, underneath the bloody cab trying to lift it up. We undid the bolts and I brought it down with me. Then when I was pushing the box up he had the nerve to tell me I wasn't pushing it high enough! I thought 'I don't need to be a mechanic to put a bolt in!' That's how I enjoyed my Sunday afternoons…

Back to playing matters, GB played Australia in the World Cup and it was an absolute fight fest—but GB won the World Cup on the try countback rule. But a few days later (9 November) Saints played them at home and absolutely battered them 37–10. We always had a good record against them and we showed we could play that night in front of 15,000 fans. Alan Whittle scored three tries and I kicked six goals. Back in those days, tour games attracted massive crowds. Everyone wanted to test themselves against the Aussies, Kiwis or the French and the games could sometimes be brutal.

Again, we cruised into the final of the Lancashire Cup beating Huyton 30–3 back in August, Swinton 20–7 (September) and Wigan in the semi final 23–0 at Central Park. That meant a match up with Alex Murphy's Leigh on 28 November at Swinton. I had kicked a couple of penalties and so had they, and in the last minute Murphy put up a towering bomb. As it dropped, Barrow positioned himself to catch it and probably win the game, but it deviated in the air and hit him straight on the head or shoulder and David Eckersley scored to win the game. Bugger…It was a bitter blow for Frank too as he had been solid that season. That gave them a 7–4 win. You know what? Two days later we beat the same team 10–4 in the BBC2 Floodlit Trophy second round.

At the beginning of December we travelled over to France to take on St Gaudens in what was billed as a European Championship. On the plane Challinor asked me if I wanted to play. I said I wasn't bothered and he told me to give it a miss. Gaudens were a bit dirty so I was glad! Both games were real brawls. It wasn't as if I was ducking out...well...I was ducking out really...perhaps they were trying to wrap me in cotton wool?

So from that moment on the plane, I knew I was going to have a good trip! I was given the job of acting Vice Chairman and one of my first acts was to put Brian Glover to bed after a big night out in Toulouse! We never used to drink pre game day so after winning the match 30–11 we celebrated. During the celebration we decided we would have to take Brian to bed and by the time we returned, he was already back behind the bar in his underpants. How he made it downstairs I will never know.

The return leg at the end of the season was a bit of a joke really. We won 62–0 after they had a night of unrivalled excess on Ormskirk Street in St Helens. That's their business I suppose but they had a big night according to the press, drank the place dry and allegedly touched up every female waitress they could find. They were banned from coming to that area of the town again and we hammered them to become European Champions.

After a replay with Wigan in the BBC2 Floodlit Trophy we played our fourth game in eight days against Leeds in the final and lost 9–5. We then played them in the second round of the Challenge Cup and lost again. Weirdly, I got a rollicking from the lads for my winning drop goal against Workington, scored with my left foot in the last minute. I remember Frank Myler coming over to me at the end of the game and asking me what I had done that for. He may have well been suggesting my drop goal attempt should have been a little wider! If we had drawn, we would have got winners' money for that, and then would have beaten them in the replay, with the resultant winner's money too! They were being a little harsh on me I thought. As a player you are tuned to win and although they had a point financially, I had to put it over.

Before that Workington game John Stephens came in from Wigan to give us a little bit more bite in the pack. He was unlucky later in his career as he was picked to go on tour and broke his leg. Eric Hughes and Geoff Pimblett also came in and Bob Blackwood got some time in the first team because Frank Wilson was injured.

It was the freshening up the team needed and we beat Leeds 22–7 in the Championship semi final to give us the chance to defend our League title against Wigan on 22 May. Although Geoff's position was stand-off, or centre in rugby union, he slotted into Frankie Barrow's fullback spot as he was injured. Wigan got off to a flyer and were 12–6 up through Ashurst who used the breeze to murder us with his touch finding. But we got back in with a shout when Blackwood flew into the corner and I booted the conversion off the touchline into the wind. It was late on in the game and I knew I had to hurry up. I didn't rush it, but I knew we had to score. I could hear the crowd—and I had to use my power. Thankfully, it went over, we were a point behind and had a couple of minutes left to put pressure on Wigan. We were down to 12 men as John Mantle had been sent off. Someone purposely had trodden on his hand and he retaliated by knocking seven bells out of him. But, a team is only down to 12 men when defending rather than attacking.

So, on our last tackle in their half, with seconds ticking down, John Walsh attempted a drop goal from miles out. It drifted wide and Billy Benyon followed it up and touched it down. Delirium. I kicked the conversion and we won. Wigan weren't happy as they claimed Benyon was offside. Looking back now, he probably was. He was on the ground, injured and then made a miraculous recovery, caught the ball and scored! Ah well…Minutes later I was lifting my first trophy as captain.

It was a less than happy occasion for my brother-in-law who had trundled home early thinking it was game over. When we finally made it home and told him we'd won, he was more than gutted!

11

'I TOOK A BIT OF TIME, MILKED IT AND IT WAS A GREAT FEELING...'

I missed out on Wembley in 1966 after hurting my hip a couple of weeks before. The venue is hardly the best place on the planet for someone who is injured with the magnitude of the Challenge Cup Final and although I tried to run off the injury, it wasn't happening. A season or two later we signed Graham Rees—a strong running second rower who we hoped would provide the platform for a cup run.

We both had to wait until 1972 to return to Wembley and that was at least five seasons too late! The Challenge Cup Final is a day for players and fans. Watching from the sidelines is hell. Those on the bench are chuffed to bits for their teammates, but don't feel part of it at all.

In 1971–72, I played 54 games as we played well in all the cup competitions. In fact, if we had won a couple more semi finals, then it would have been a longer season! You know what? I didn't think that was a lot though. The whole point of playing was to get into finals. You couldn't get into the finals and complain about the amount of games you had to play in because that was the point after all! I didn't realise I was playing in so many games because I couldn't have felt any fitter. As a team we just wanted to win every game possible, and because, in all honesty, we only got paid when we won games anyway.

So we began that season with four 'cup' games. We beat Leigh and Warrington in the Lancashire Cup, then Leigh once more in the Charity Shield. Our fourth game on 17 August was the Lancashire Cup semi final against Widnes. But we lost 12–10 to start the season off with a whimper. We thought we were going to win and were definitely favourites, but I don't think we realised what a difficult game it was going to be. The conditions were bad, as they always seemed to be back in those days.

A few months later in December we picked up the BBC2 Floodlit Trophy by beating Rochdale 8–2. Again, we were overwhelming favourites but Frank Myler had joined them as player-coach. Any side he coached was always going to be tough to break down and, of course, he knew us inside out. Myler was a good player himself, as well as an organiser and dictator. I'd been at the club for 10 years and to been seen on TV winning the trophy was great. The folks back home watching on telly saw it too. Yet, four days later we lost the John Player Trophy semi final to Wakefield.

Those little knocks kept us going all season and as the games racked up, we became more confident that Wembley was a real option. We struggled past Oldham in the first round, then thumped Huddersfield and York in the next two to set up a semi final with Murphy's Warrington. I kicked two goals with Walsh and Heaton dropping goals but we were losing 10–8. We won a penalty around 30 yards out and I fancied a pop. Their scrum half was on the mark giving me a bit of lip and I booted it over. Before it had even gone between the uprights, I told him to have a look at it going over!

Sledging happened a bit in those days but it was never nasty. I remember Eric Ashton talking me into playing prop towards the end of my Saints' career on the proviso it was no different to playing at loose forward. It was just a number on the shirt, he said. Well, I played in that position against Oldham and as we packed down Barry Kear asked: 'What ya doing here Kelvin?' And after the first scrum I was asking myself: 'What am I doing here Kelvin?' Talk about pain. He was pinching me and one of their props said I could do it back. I tried but I had tears streaming down my face and told him I was trying! I wondered what the hell I was doing there.

Anyway, the semi final finished 10 apiece and a few days later we were back at Central Park for the replay. In front of 32,000 we fought out another close game. There were loads of Warrington fans in the crowd that day and they were leading once again until Stephens broke through, went around the fullback, and passed to me for a try—one of eight I would score that season. The crowd went quiet and we were on our way to Wembley. Winning a semi is so important as when you get to the final, you have that final day. Losing in a semi means you come nowhere.

As well as the final against Leeds on 13 May, we had a Championship semi final against Bradford to play on 4 May and we hoped we wouldn't get any injuries—much like in 1966 when Hull KR gave us a battering in the Championship semi. And so, as is par the course, Tony Karalius and Eric Prescott got injured. I have to admit that in the back of my mind I was thinking about when I got injured against Hull KR. During the game I can't remember worrying about being injured, but it was a tough game and once I was in the thick of it, I forgot all about it. That meant both Tony and Eric were given late fitness tests during the week and Challinor did not name the team until then either. In the end, he called up Les Greenall for the final. Les had hardly played that season…what a stand up for him!

Preparations for a Challenge Cup Final haven't changed much over the years and this was no exception. Before we headed off to our training camp at Selsdon Park Hotel there was a massive fireworks display that made the event feel all the more special. Sunderland had stayed at Selsdon and they had won the cup so that was a nice omen. During the week, we went through a few moves and stayed off the beer. Drinking was never in the equation…well, I shouldn't say never but we knew Leeds were going to be a tough nut to crack.

The side was full of internationals and had won the league by six points too. Alan Hardisty and I did a show with Eddie Waring over in Yorkshire before the game. He had a hotel room in Leeds and the focus of the show was typically about how good Leeds were. We knew that and were clearly heading into the game as underdogs.

By the Thursday before the game, Challinor had still not named the team because of fitness tests and we only found out the day before who was going to turn out. The lads picked up some tweaks that week too, which really disrupted our flow and made the team selection a bit of a shambles really. As John Mantle picked his kids up from school, someone whacked him in his car, leaving him with 12 stitches in his head even before we came down to the camp. Heaton damaged his ankle, Chisnall injured his thigh and Stephens hurt his neck too. But it would have taken something really bad to keep them off the field. So, eventually, Challinor went with Geoff Pimblett; Les Jones, Bill Benyon, John Walsh, Frank Wilson; Ken Kelly, Geoff Heaton; Graham Rees, Les Greenall, John Stephens, John Mantle, Eric Chisnall, Kel Coslett. Subs: Alan Whittle, Kelvin Earl.

Geoff [Pimblett] was playing well that season and had made

several outstanding tackles during the earlier rounds to keep us in the cup. Jones could score for fun. Benyon was one of the best in the league at the time and had been at the club since he was 17. He was now 27 and in his prime. Walsh was a natural player with great ability. Kelly was a youngster but had proved himself and was worthy of a place and together with Heaton they could change a game. Heaton was like Keith Hepworth. In terms of ability, both were quite similar. There was nothing between them except that one played for GB and the other didn't.

Graham Rees was bought from Swinton to get us to Wembley and he had finally made it! He was a strong running second rower. Greenhall was no slouch and he never let the team down. Stephens had scored in the semi final and was a vital cog in a pack that never stopped motoring. Mantle and Chisnall could have been in anyone's pack in any era. You can't speak any higher than that. You would pick them and wouldn't be disappointed. On the bench were Earl and Whittle—one young, one a little more experienced.

Coming into Wembley on the team coach with the police escort makes the whole event feel very special. Why should teams have to worry about how to get there? In my current role at Saints I make sure we get an escort to finals as it makes everything so much easier. Teams know that no one else is going down the road other than the other finalists and that's what cup finals are all about. They are special days and because players have watched finals on TV in the past, suddenly to be in a final is an amazing experience.

Once inside, you are in match mode. You get to have a look at the pitch and see how big Wembley is. You take it all in and I know it is a cliché, but you feel the history of the place—and that brings a little bit of pressure. But back in the dressing room with the massive baths and the air of expectation, that disappears.

One thing I remember is there was no team talk whatsoever from Challinor. I think I was the only one to give a team talk and I went to each player in turn. I didn't give them a big sermon; just spoke a few words of encouragement here and there. It was up to us to help each other. I spoke to Greenhall and Kelly and used their, and my, nerves as an excuse to help everyone else.

Once the call goes up from the referee, you make your way into the tunnel. I read recently that Geoff Pimblett was quoted after the game as saying he expected to lose—or at least there were some doubts. I understand why he said that, but I don't think he went out there expecting to be beaten. No one does that. We didn't know the team until Friday night because of the fitness tests and that meant we had some other things still in the back of our minds. Bringing youngsters into the team perhaps took our minds off the opposition and relaxed us a little bit.

In the tunnel, you jump up and down to stay loose, and then you move forward. In the tunnel you are at the bottom and don't hear the noise until you get out. The noise just hits you. Some players try to spot family in the crowd, others get settled. As we approached the half way line we lined up and I introduced the team to the American Ambassador. I can't remember his name but he was a nice fella! Then, after the anthem, we peeled off one at a time as our name was read out.

What do I remember of the game? Well, after joining the club to get us to Wembley, Rees scored two minutes into the game and before 3 p.m. So you could say that is the quickest ever Cup Final try. He charged down a kick and scored and I kicked the conversion. We never lost the lead after that and that kept us fresh. Playing in front is always a damn sight better than trying to catch up!

As usual, conditions were wet and miserable and the ball was slippery. There were chances to take on both sides and Leeds had to take them because we were ahead. And that's the reason I dropped a goal to keep us in front in the second half: we went further ahead to make them score. We went in six up at half time and caught our breaths. Then Cookson scored in the first minute of the second half under the sticks and I rollicked John Stephens for missing him. I was covering Ray Batten, their loose forward and he didn't pick Cookson up. He came in from one side and Barton popped it up. Thankfully, they missed the goal under the sticks and we stayed ahead. My second half drop goal was huge and it went about 10 yards over the sticks too. There was no way back for Leeds then as our defence was just too good. When the whistle went, Jim ran onto the pitch with Eddie Cheetham and we were all delighted, as we weren't supposed to win. Leeds were a class act and it was a bit of a shock.

It seemed like an age before I went up the steps to pick up the cup. I was young and fit, but I was bloody knackered by the time I got up those steps to meet the dignitaries. By the time I'd finished the handshakes, I just wanted to get the trophy aloft! I wanted to do everything right and not drop the trophy or its lid. I didn't want to make a hash of it. If I'd just turned and lifted it, some players may not have made it up the endless steps so I waited a little while.

Then came the moment! It is the captain's moment as well as the fans' moment too. I had watched this moment on TV a number of times and it was something I wanted to do myself from being a schoolboy. Kids play act lifting up a cup don't they? So…I took a bit of time and milked it and it was a great feeling! As I walked down the steps with the cup, everyone was tapping me on the back and my brother was sat there too. When we got into the dressing room later, my dad had managed to talk himself in. The fact he got to London was a miracle in itself, so we had a picture taken of us both having a glass of champagne. It was absolutely great.

Once down on the pitch, players do a lap of honour for the fans and the other players. As captain you give up the trophy and just soak it all in. It is a great occasion and something I still enjoy now. I waited a long time to do it and I'm glad I got the chance. Nobody can take that away from you.

After the game, Frank Bough told me in the tunnel that I had also won the Lance Todd trophy as man of the match. I got six quid for winning it! Winning seems to be more important these days as you get to attend a big dinner afterwards at the Willows in Salford and a lot of money. Back then the Red Devils' committee who organised the event awarded the trophy and it was more of a gesture rather than the accolade that the press vote on now.

I also made a comment to Frank that 'Chisy could have his chips' now the game was over. Eric Chisnall liked his pie and chips and Challinor banned them in the lead up to the game from Thursday. He had been hankering for them and was happy when he got his hands on them later. I was just glad to get there and win. We just wanted to play, get in front and when we did, hold out to win. We did a lot of defending and everyone expected Leeds to score. The post match banquet at the Selsdon was superb with the players and their wives as well as club officials having a few beers, speeches and a bloody good singsong.

Our arrival back in Lime Street was low key until we came through Huyton and Old Swan on the open top bus to find people either side. When we got back to the town hall it was totally chocker! After more speeches had been made, we had a few beers and went our separate ways. It was a great feeling, but we had a game the following Saturday against Leeds in the Championship Final and we needed to start afresh once again. Leeds won that game by four points, showing how close the two teams were throughout the season.

Incidentally, we were given maroon blazers to wear at Wembley and although I don't know why I did it now, I took mine down to my mother's after the Final to show my mum and dad. Jacqueline and I decided to go into Swansea for some lunch and it was throwing it down, so I took the blazer. I was coming out of the car park in town, taking a left turn in front of a hotel and the first person I spoke to was Tony Fisher and his wife, who I played against on the Saturday. He took one look at me and I'll never forget the words he uttered: 'You posing bastard.' I thought what a greeting by a fellow Welshman! It took me 20 minutes to apologise and I took the blazer back to the car embarrassed and then gave it to my father-in-law! He was only five foot six inches and a collier born in Thatto Heath, but he wore it for years.

Perhaps the rugby gods were unhappy with my blatant posing as a season later we failed to hit the highs of our cup winning form. We brought in Georgie Nichols from Widnes and Roy Mathias from Llanelli. Once again I was sent down to Wales to 'woo' Roy into signing, Mathias says I wasn't much help at all, but he signed so I must have said the right things. As I had with Warlow all those years back, I told him about the club and impressed on him that you only got one bite of the cherry and that meant getting as much money as he could.

He's known as Honest Roy these days. He has his own businesses and rents out a few houses and pool tables, that sort of thing. He was in the pub business; he has kept himself busy since he retired as that's his character and he is honest! And that's his problem! He did well for the club, scoring on his debut against Warrington. But that 1972–73 season was strange as we came off such a positive year being Cup Final winners, yet failed to really move on or evolve as such from that winning team. We played in semi finals rather than finals which was disappointing. It was also the first team that Challinor had the opportunity to put his own stamp on and we didn't get going.

Georgie Nic wanted to play loose forward but Harry Cook told him that he wasn't guaranteed a loose forward position if he joined the club. I think Challinor wanted him to play there so he picked him for Great Britain at loose forward, even though I was the regular at Saints. George was injured in March and I think that made Jim's choice a little easier. In fact, I missed one game that season, playing the rest at loose and twice in the second row. The pack shuffled around a bit and I was really the only constant face. I always remember Georgie Nic's first game as we beat Leeds 5–2 at Headingley on 20 January. It was dreadful weather and we'd suffered hail stones and everything else the weather could throw at us. Tony Karalius jumped straight in the bath afterwards still wearing boots, shorts, socks, jersey, the works.

There were also some fresh faces in the half backs too. Dave Eckersley could play everywhere—he was a utility back who could play stand off and fullback, and he played a couple at centre that season. Ken Kelly, Heaton and Alan Gwilliam were also in the mix. That meant four players were, in effect, battling for two places. That was never going to work! Eric Prescott left the club for £12,000 and you can't blame the Board for cashing in on a promising player. Mick Murphy came into the pack too.

With Mel James, Georgie Nic and Mathias there was a potential changing of the guard at the club as we pushed forward for more honours. We also looked at Barry John and Tommy David from Wales. Harry Cook asked me about both of them, as was the style in those days. They asked directly whether I thought someone could join the club. I might have been cutting my nose off though, as Tommy David could have played loose and some of the other players the club looked at could also kick goals! So it was difficult for me to give a straight answer. Barry John was a star, as was David, but they were both playing union for Wales at the time and turned the club down. It was probably a difficult decision for those guys to make.

There were some good players in Wales and when they got a team in Cardiff, it had the real potential to grow. But they chose big name players who were probably a couple of years too far gone. The spectators down there compared those players to how they played in their pomp and they weren't winning games either. The game remained static there as a result. At least with the Crusaders now, they have three years with the new League franchise system to build something. They can bring youngsters into the game and build on that to establish the game in Wales.

But as I say, that year was a transition season at the Saints. We lost to Widnes in the Lancashire Cup second round, to Leeds in the BBC2 Floodlit Trophy and the John Player Trophy and then to Wigan in the Challenge Cup second round. Then, Leeds yet again—obviously a bit pissed from the year before—beat us 7–2 in the Championship semi final.

Weirdly, the 1973–74 season continued in much the same vain and the club was losing a bit of money off the pitch too. I read recently that I was at the top of Leigh's shortlist for their vacant player-coach position, but I have to say I can't remember that. I was still a young man and playing so there's no way I would have gone over to coach. That wasn't correct; I didn't apply or at least I can't remember doing so anyway!

I played in the second row a lot during the beginning of the season, and then moved back to loose forward in mid October. But on 22 December in Featherstone, I was caught with an elbow that smashed my nose in two. It happened a few minutes before the end of the first half. I saw John Stephens going in under the sticks something like 50 yards away and next thing an elbow hit and pushed my nose across towards my ear. Their prop, Les Tonks, had blatantly smashed my face with his elbow.

I don't mind players using fists and things like that so much, but using an elbow is low and violent. Unfortunately none of my teammates managed to land one back on him. I had to come off, although I didn't want to and perhaps I was disorientated as I had a go at our trainer for trying to take my boots off. When the lads came in at 8–4 down, they took one look at the trainer trying to take my boots off, then one look at my face. One said: 'Don't look in the mirror Kel, for Christ's sake,' so of course I did exactly the opposite. My nose was spread right across my face in varying shades of black and blue.

I went straight to Pontefract Hospital in the afternoon and as it was Christmas no one was there so they couldn't do anything. They said there was no point in me staying in over Christmas and told me to go home. I went back to Featherstone and got on the coach. Fair play to the club, they called St Helens Hospital to arrange for me to see someone.

The coach pulled up at the hospital. I saw Jimmy Heron the specialist and he told me to come in on Christmas Eve. So I spent the next couple of days in agony until I could get my nose fixed. On Christmas Eve morning as I went to the hospital I passed my wagon parked in its yard and noticed out of the corner of my eye that the bloody thing had a flat tyre. As I was late for my appointment, I went in. The consultant asked me what type of nose I wanted, Roman or whatever. Then they opened a theatre especially for me, fixed my nose, plugged it and whacked a bandage round. On the way home I stopped at the wagon and fixed the tyre! I wanted to fix it before the holidays began. It would just have been on my mind. I missed four games with the injury to my nose, sat on the bench for the fifth and was then back at loose forward against Rochdale on 20 January.

That season, Jim Challinor resigned from the club around March time to continue with his GB role. He said in the press that the GB team were crying out for a decent loose forward and he said that I was half his team at Saints. I always wondered why he said that and I still didn't get a shot. I always felt I could do a good job for GB, but I knew there were always the likes of George Nicholls, Malcolm Reilly and Dave Robinson waiting in the background. Those players appeared regularly for their clubs and weren't the sort of lads who would have a bad day to give another player a sniff.

Reilly was picked ahead of me in the end. I know the press and Jim thought we were a little weak at loose but what was wrong with Dougie Laughton, Reilly or Nic? We were all worth our weight in gold. But, I thought I was worth a punt in that mix. I thought my goal kicking would have given me the edge too. If Jim thought that I could do a job and that I was half his team, then surely he should have given me the chance. When he ran up to me in training and said I'd missed out by a vote and that he was sorry, I knew it was all rubbish.

Ironically, I found a picture of me wearing a GB blazer with that season's date on the back. I wonder if I got the badge and blazer for being on reserve? In the early sixties there had been fierce competition for the fullback spot and I was on reserve until I broke my leg which put me right back. I have a picture of me with Mick Murphy and I am coming into my own at loose forward. I still wonder if I was not supposed to have this blazer and that now you have read this I'll be in trouble! I may well get a letter at some point for obtaining a blazer under false pretences, so don't tell anyone!

Although I had my testimonial that season, I didn't think I was too old to go on tour. I had played for around 12 years and came out of the testimonial season with around £4,000. I thoroughly enjoyed my testimonial season. There were concert nights in social clubs and for doing them I earned £100. Les Jones had a testimonial after me and earned something like £30,000. How come he earned so much in comparison to me? I think it was because the dinners started and there were also benefit matches. I asked for a testimonial game and Harry Cook said the league wouldn't let me have one as we couldn't have a game within 30 days of the season starting and ending. Whether that was an excuse or a genuine reason I don't know.

Some people think testimonials are a waste of time but they reward players who stay loyal to a club. If players change clubs, they are likely to get a signing on fee and such. Whilst players should get as much as they can, it can be an unfair advantage to move on, because then loyalty isn't rewarded. I got £4,000 for 12 years' service, whereas players who move three or four times could get a fee each time. I'm not saying that is wrong though!

I know that testimonials are worth big money these days. But if players move on and get paid, then why shouldn't players who stay loyal to a club also be rewarded? I suppose players show more loyalty these days too. Players can come in, take the money and then leave.

As I said, Jim resigned from the club in March, ended up at Oldham and stayed coach of GB for a while. The Saints had the best record from 1966–74, finishing no lower than third in all those years. Unfortunately we just couldn't win the league. In Jim's final season we were one draw either side of winning the league over Salford. We never hit the highs of 1972 and spent some serious money bringing players in.

That team was well capable of winning the league too. Mathias, Benyon, Pimblett and Bobby Goulding's dad Bob played too. He was a doorman who had played at Huyton. He spoke to me years after about a game we played. He said I had the ball, made a bit of a break and I passed it on the outside to Mathias and he said I could have passed it on the inside to him. He claims this showed I didn't like him. Incidentally Mathias did score from my pass. John Warlow was enticed back too. In a cup tie against Rochdale he'd had a hard physical match and we realised he could come back and do a good job for us!

We beat Australia 11–7 in November when I did Whitaker. We kept on the blind side all night as conditions were so bad and they couldn't cope. I ran on to Whitaker and whacked him with a big stiff arm…accidentally of course. He hit the deck and I innocently wondered what was wrong with him. Then a couple of weeks later we lost 13–12 in the semi of the BBC2 Floodlit Trophy.

These are just examples of the games that epitomised our season. We had been reaching finals for 25 years in a row then suddenly we weren't reaching finals quite as much anymore. I can't say why, but we just couldn't seem to get over the line. In previous years we would have won both the BBC2 Floodlit Trophy semi and the John Players Trophy semi against Warrington. I'm not criticising anyone, it could have been anyone's fault but the 1966 team were difficult to beat and that's why they went 20-odd games undefeated. The early seventies team did the same and we kind of lost that edge.

I remember trying a drop goal from 45 yards out in the Merit Championship Final game at the end of the season and it drifted off to the left. In previous seasons it would have drifted left and then come back right. We weren't experiencing the same lucky breaks anymore—that can sometimes happen with a team. That missed kick made the difference between winning and losing 13–12 to Warrington as we eventually did.

Although we didn't win anything, we still got to the Final. If you look back, that isn't too bad, is it?

12

'THE FOUNDATIONS WERE THERE...'

I know I have been hard on Jim Challinor. We were probably more successful under Jim than at any other time, bar 1966, in my St Helens' career. Yet, I maintain the success we had was down to the quality of players and the moves that came across from Cliff Evans' day. Jim never suggested anything to me or asked my advice and as his captain, I did the team talk before various games in his tenure at the Saints.

Eric Ashton was different. He communicated with his captain and senior professionals. He listened and decided whether to take our advice but at least he sought out our opinions and that made a big difference. As I said earlier, my main memory of Challinor was Mantle coming to me on the day of the Barrow game asking if he was going to play. When I went into coaching, I took this on board and decided always to discuss things with the team. I always named the line up as early as I could so everyone knew where they stood. We could then approach the game and the opposition in plenty of time.

Everyone who knows me knows how close I was to Eric. That didn't necessarily mean I was so close that I didn't or couldn't criticise him or have an opinion on him. When my coaching contract at Saints wasn't renewed, he had just come on the

Board and he abstained on his first Board meeting. Tom Ellard did the same. Stan Ince voted for me. Eric Latham apologised that he couldn't make the meeting. I think that is twollap! The abstentions did me no favours and they might have well voted against it as it meant the same thing in the end, but that's for another chapter.

The team knew what Eric was about. He was a legend at Wigan. I must have played against Billy Boston and him for around six years. They were an awesome partnership and could open up teams at will. They were quick, gifted and could also defend. Eric was a real professional who loved the game. You knew what you were getting with him—and that simply was a professional attitude. He fined players who were late for meetings and training, and I remember one incident in France when he fined a couple of the lads for being late. He called a meeting for 12 p.m., and some bastard locked me and Ash in our rooms. By the time we got out of our rooms, we were around 20 minutes late and most of the players were waiting for us. They demanded fines and such!

He held the record for captaining teams at Wembley and was a GB captain too. He had an OBE and was highly thought of in all rugby league circles. Above all, he was a St Helens lad and always wanted to be a part of the club. When the chance came up, he had a lot of friends in the town and on the Board of Directors so he took his chance. When he was in his pomp the club went for him and offered a record price for a transfer. That was in 1961, but in the end they signed Mick Sullivan instead. He wanted to play for St Helens, but it didn't happen.

Quite simply, he brought stability, communication and common sense to the Saints. He was an ambassador for the sport and gave the team confidence as a result. He involved me more than any other coach I had played for. There's no way he would have left an international like John Mantle still wondering if he was playing on the way up to a game.

Eric didn't have to do much with us at training, but he got us to believe we could beat teams again and that season we did—sweeping to the League title by nine points in 30 games over Wigan. Perhaps the real difference was that the things that went wrong in games last season, went right that season. Perhaps it was down to luck or perhaps it was down to belief. I don't know.

We were still a team not afraid to try new moves on the field utilising the fitness that Joe Coan had begun and Eddie Cheetham had continued. Eric had a tremendous rugby brain and that stuck with us to the end of our playing days. I remember sitting with Geoff Pimblett, Ash and the coach of Eastern Suburbs who hammered us in the World Club Challenge in 1976. He was amazed with the number of moves we had put on and wanted to know where they had come from.

I know this all sounds straight down the line, but we still had some fun. Although the game was becoming professional in terms of attitude, it wasn't as if we weren't allowed to have fun! It was always looked at as a professional game. We always put it at the top of our priorities; it was just that we had another job to do as well, whether that involved lifting spuds like Tommy Bishop or changing wagon tyres just after having your nose fixed like me. The secret was to be fit enough to keep picking ourselves up each time—especially as we were paid for playing!

We won the league that season after failing to do so for a number of previous seasons. It's difficult to explain why we started winning the big games and titles once more. Did naming the team early make a difference between winning and losing? Eric named the team early and that meant we could focus on the opposition and gave us time to work out how to beat them. Perhaps this focus took us forward.

I'm making it sound like we swept everything before us in 1974–75, but that wasn't the case. Yes, we won the league but we were in bad form in the cup competitions. We went out of the Lancashire Cup early doors to Workington and lost the BBC2 Floodlit Trophy to Salford. Our Challenge Cup campaign ended early at Wakefield. Our Premiership campaign was good though, but a ruthless Leeds beat us in the Final 26–11 after being 16–0 up at half time. What I am saying is that the foundations were being laid.

The team hadn't changed that much either, Ashton had the same players as Challinor. Eddie Cunningham came in for £5,000, Warlow was still around, but we retained a good core of players. A second rower by trade, Eddie played at centre that season against Bradford and I remember Ash coming over to me saying we might have a problem. He said Eddie wasn't happy as he thought he was tackling too much. I asked Ash if that was a problem as if he didn't tackle, then he didn't play.

These days there are three men in a tackle, but back then we used to say one player tackled and the rest would leave well alone and wait for the next play. That's what happened with Cunningham, we took responsibility for who we were tackling and he didn't like it. He wanted to run in the tries instead! Once the communication was up and running on the field, he fell in line.

Georgie Nicholls won Man of Steel in 1978 and he deserved it. He played in the second row and was a tremendous forward with a good engine. But he was also part of a side that would go all day. Mantle, Chisnall and Cunningham would keep on going for you. Mel James was another strong player and Coslett could motor a bit if you let him…

13

'THERE WAS RUGBY LEAGUE IN WALES AND IT WAS THRIVING...'

Appearing for your country is simply the pinnacle of any player's career. For a village boy coming up from the valleys, passion for the country of your birth is strong. Playing rugby union for Wales gave me an intense feeling of pride and doing the same in rugby league meant I joined a select group of players classed as dual internationals.

Wales always had a rugby league team, but its fixtures were few and far between. We played two or three times a season for a couple of years, then for some reason the games would stop. A couple of years later it would start up again. That made recognition for the team hard and establishing the game in Wales difficult. So it was with great delight that GB was disbanded and the four nations split for the 1975 World Cup. Looking back now I wonder whether I would have been picked to play for Great Britain if the nations hadn't been split. Ste Norton played for England and if players were better than him then they had a shot in the GB team. However it was always good to play for Wales and represent my country.

As I have said before, I always felt that I had to produce the goods to show the rest of the world how strong Welsh rugby was. I always needed to prove to people we, as a country, were worthy of a place in the World Cup. It was important for Wales to go into the competition even if some of the players wouldn't play for Great Britain. Personally, I thought the likes of Millsy [Jim Mills], Watkins, Fisher, Sullivan, Cunningham, Nicholas and Willicombe played well for GB. In my view, a combined Wales and England team could have won the World Cup that year. Australia didn't beat England, but we did, and that shows the talent and capability that was there.

Anyway, back to the tournament itself. In a fit of madness that can often befall our great sport, the powers that be decided to split the competition and run it over eight months. There would be a period of games over in France, Australia and New Zealand, and then we would come back to the UK. I thought it wasn't a good thing to spread the competition out over eight months because people lost interest and the anticipation of it all. There couldn't be a concurrent team as players picked up injuries and how could you peak as a team over a spell of eight months? Especially if you were in a team like Wales with our aging players. The time period was just too long. In effect, the competition spanned two seasons.

At least in the most recent World Cup, players spent five weeks in one place. All the players were out there, training together and good to go. In 1975, it was a hit and miss thing really, and for me, whilst it was a tremendous experience, it was a miss. It became more of a World Cup when we were over in Australia and New Zealand. We were with our teammates for five weeks and that was the important thing. As the tournament was split over eight months, we didn't feel the magnitude of the event or the volume of it. Although we did have some good attendances over in Swansea, it wasn't the same as it had been over in Oz and New Zealand previously. Our World Cup didn't start until we beat England in Brisbane.

We were continually selling the game in Wales and we always felt the pressure to do well to show the rest of the rugby league community that rugby league in Wales was thriving. The World Cup was just a game and we didn't realise the urgency of it until we got out there and played games with the Welsh badge on our chests.

Ron Simpson was the Welsh team manager and Les Pearce was the coach. I was vice captain to Dai Watkins. After losing to France 14–7 in Toulouse on 2 March, our next game was in Brisbane on 10 June against England. Ron and Les chose the team to go on tour and it had talent, even though we were a little long in the tooth.

The squad was: Peter Banner (Salford), Brian Butler (Swinton), Kel Coslett (St Helens), Eddie Cunningham (St Helens), Colin Dixon (Salford), Richard Evans (Swinton), Tony Fisher (Leeds), Bill Francis (Wigan), John Mantle (St Helens), Roy Mathias (St Helens), Jim Mills (Widnes), Mike Nicholas (Warrington), Peter Rowe (Blackpool Borough), Clive Sullivan (Hull Kingston Rovers), David Treasure (Oldham), Glyn Turner (Hull Kingston Rovers), Bobby Wanbon (Warrington), David Watkins (Salford), David Willicombe (Wigan) and Frank Wilson (St Helens).

That team was probably a couple of years older than perhaps it should have been. It had real ability within it and was very capable of winning big games. But, with ageing limbs, we needed more time to recover. This could have been an excuse for not winning more games, but if on average we had been 18-months younger we would have recovered better. We could have gone that little bit further and been a little bit quicker. Even with all this in mind, we shouldn't have been playing test matches within a couple of days of each other as we did in that tournament. Especially as the tournament was spread out over eight bloody months!

I was probably getting a bit long in the tooth myself at this point, but my legs were good and my engine was still strong. I wasn't thinking of retirement but it was on my mind to take my game year by year. When Saints lost to Wakefield in the third round of the Challenge Cup, thoughts of retiring did start to appear. Les Jones scored and ref Mickey Norton from Widnes pulled us back for a forward pass. I thought then and there that I'd had enough of this. But playing for Wales in the World Cup kept me going. It set me up for another season.

There was genuine belief in the Welsh team that we could win the World Cup. Daft as it sounds, we recorded a couple of songs at the Magnum Studios in Hyde. The nominated singers were Jim Mills, Les Pearce, Ron Simpson, Colin Dixon, Tony Fisher and me and we were due in the studio at 9 a.m. After an hour or two we weren't singing well at all—so we went over the road for a beer or two. A few hours later we went back and absolutely murdered the tune.

We always thought we could win and whenever we played we had a great following. It made us feel very special as players and as a vice captain. We felt we had to prove ourselves and when we headed home, we wanted to show our fans that we didn't have to play rugby union and could play rugby league. When we wore our Welsh suit, we truly believed we were going to win. We weren't just going over for a jolly.

We got off to a flyer, beating England 12–7 at Lang Park in Brisbane. It was a tight match but I always thought we had the better of them. Afterwards we had a few beers to celebrate and a real bouncing evening. Our next game was against Australia in Sydney four days later. Games against Australia were always tight and whenever Saints played them in tour games we were capable of beating them. Giving us four days to prepare for our next test match was nothing short of criminal. We had just beaten England on the Tuesday and were a little excited after the win. Given our average team age, this schedule made recovery time an issue. It took us a while to get to Sydney on the Wednesday, and we then had a day or so to prepare for our biggest game of the tournament against Australia. We missed out on the build up. Consequently we were 10–0 down before we got on the park and the team never really got going. Eventually we lost 30–13. It was a blow as with more time to prepare we could have beaten the Aussies.

Our next match was against New Zealand in Carlaw Park in Auckland on 28 June and we were just edged in New Zealand's 13–8 win. At points in the game, we could have taken them and we were a credit to ourselves.

At various points during our tour of Australia and New Zealand we played a few friendlies to get our eye in. Before playing the Kiwis we played in Greymouth and won 35–5. There was a brawl after a few minutes and Millsy went in to sort it out. Then, on 2 November, he stood all over Greengrass in our win over New Zealand in Swansea. I had injured my ribs beforehand and didn't play so I can't remember much about it. Mathias told me it was bad and it came more out of annoyance at the fact he had just scored! Apparently both Mills and Greengrass are talking again and are actually friends.

There was always aggro when Wales were in town. If you look at the team on paper it's obvious we were a physical side. We had to be. That was our forte—meet them up front then Watkins and co can do their stuff on the outside. Jim Mills had a reputation for being sent off. I think I'm right in saying he had more sending offs in international rugby than any other player. But when he played for us, he only used to pile in for retaliation—he was never the aggressor. If you look at his record, the vast majority of those sending offs were for retaliation.

When he attacked the player in Greymouth in one of our tour games, he did it because the person he smacked had hit David Treasure, our half back. When we beat the West Coast, their big man was a 6ft 1 second rower. Millsy clobbered him because he did our player. It all went off and just as I was heading in to help, Colin Dixon said to me: 'Don't go Kel, I think he's killed him.'

I suppose sometimes we lost the plot when we made games too physical. When a chap is sent off Plan A goes out of the window. We weren't dirty though. The press said Jim brought the game into disrepute, but all the Aussie clubs tapped him up when he was over there. He was well respected.

Mills was playing for North Sydney when the Lions were over in the early seventies. Terry Price was fullback at the time and after being injured was kept in hospital. Millsy went to visit him, as the Lions had gone to New Zealand and on his third visit, the sister collared him outside the ward. She demanded to know who was visiting Terry. Millsy admitted he was and the sister said she'd cleaned up around Terry's bed that morning, opened his locker and two dozen empty Guinness cans fell out. She asked if Millsy had done that, and although he had a carrier bag under his arm full of cans at the time, denied it was him!

The game at Greymouth had been an evening kick off and to cheer up Millsy after his sending off, Butler, Mathias and I took him for a few beers afterwards. We were staying in a big pub called The Wellington. We were leaving at quarter to five or six in the morning and heading for Auckland. The more beers we had, the noisier we became. Then the landlord gave us crayfish—especially when the lads started coming back in from a night around the town.

Les Pearce had gone to bed early and the increasing noise levels made him come down. He said: 'I'm fed up listening to you sing, I've been in bed an hour and can't sleep, so I'm joining you.' He stayed with us until we went the following morning. Dai Watkins got quite ill on the tour after the test in Auckland. We played New Zealand and visited a vineyard on the Monday before playing Whatuira on the Wednesday. It was the last game of the tour so Les Pearce took us for a treat. Ronnie Simpson said: 'I know it is the last game, but no drinking before it.' So as a party we asked what was the point of us going to a vineyard at all? We got dragged along to see the copper vats, looked at wine bottles lined up on tables and weren't allowed a drop. We did the tour at midday, missing out the vines, and Clive Sullivan kept asking questions and prolonging the agony and exit so to speak.

By around 1 p.m., Les Pearce and Ron Simpson were fed up of Clive so they let us have a sip of wine. We were told not to over indulge and to be polite. By 8 p.m. some of the lads were in a bad way; Watkins missed the game through wine poisoning. When we got to the hotel, Ronnie had to climb up the stairs to bed on his hands and knees.

Whilst in Auckland we trained in the most barren place on a field next to a cemetery. One particular day, I'm not sure if it was before the test match or before the Auckland game, it was raining and misty. We all tipped up, booting the ball around and noticed there was a big funeral taking place. When we had finished the session and looked into the game scenarios and the moves, Les Pearce gave us a good talking to. Picture this, we were out in the countryside, in a field with a funeral taking place next door. The only people talking at the time were Les Pearce and the vicar doing his sermon. Les got a bit excited and he started effing and blinding. A couple of the lads said, 'Hang on Les, there's a chap getting buried here!'

Les said: 'He can't hear me. He's dead.'

We had a great time on the tour, but we worked hard as well. We were committed from day one. There was always loads of banter—especially when Alex Murphy mouthed off saying he was training rabbits and we were dogs before the England game. It got worse when we beat them, and we effectively robbed them of the World Cup. We gave it our all and certainly enjoyed it.

If the tournament had lasted five or six weeks instead of eight months it would have been great. We played a lot of tour games too, but I didn't mind playing that many—that's what we went on tour for. It was a fairly successful tour that we were worthy of, and if we had beaten New Zealand we would have been okay.

Of course, being away from home was difficult. I had a wife, three kids, plus a haulage business and the impetus fell on Jacqueline to cope with it all. It was a long trip, so I was glad to get home by the end of it.

In the remaining four fixtures of the World Cup on these shores, we beat New Zealand 25–24 and France 23–2. But we lost to England 22–16 and Australia 18–6 in Swansea. It meant we finished third in the tournament with three wins from eight games. Australia won it despite failing to beat England.

14

'DAD'S ARMY
INDEED...'

The World Cup had given me the impetus to stave off retiring for another year. I think when I started the 1974–75 season I was ready to finish. I wanted to go to the World Cup and that was such a good experience that afterwards I decided I wanted to do another year. I'm glad I did. I think deep down, though, I knew this would be my last season as a player.

I began pretty much as I always had, kicking them over for fun and playing well at loose forward. Midway through the season—around February 1976 I agreed to play at prop against Hull in the first round of the Challenge Cup. I did it really for Eric. We talked about it over Christmas and we thought it would be okay. He told me it wouldn't be very different; the only difference would be the number on the shirt. It was the biggest lie he ever told me. Playing at prop was for the team. You had to scrummage in those days and it was bloody hard work too. That first game was hard, as you had to hold your corner and help your hooker. It brought a few tears to my eyes in those first few games to be honest. It was beneficial for the club, although it meant David Hull played loose forward instead of Mel James who was on the bench in the Challenge Cup Final.

I wasn't built like a prop forward but I had a lot of help from

John Mantle and Tony Karalius as they told me what they wanted and needed to happen. Hookers need to be comfortable so I must have done all right as they kept me playing and Tony kept firing the ball over for me to take it in. Mantle, Tony and I stayed around the rucks and allowed the youngsters to run about in the clear space. It seemed to work all right. There were good players in the team so it wasn't too difficult a transition for me.

There was such confidence in that team though. We weren't worried about one to one marking and could leave the tackling to one man. Of course we had to keep an eye on people coming off them, but we had confidence in our own teammates. We could get set as the others tackled. Of course, the team was a year older, but it was an incredible year for trophies. A few of us had come back from Oz and we were getting on a bit, but we had the confidence and had been together for a number of years. We knew it was a team effort and we all played for each other.

The fans always got behind us. On 15 September 1974 we travelled to Dewsbury and won, but beforehand we broke down on the motorway. Supporters in cars and a number of buses stopped and gave members of the team a lift to the ground. We all arrived at Dewsbury at different times but at least we got there. Ironically, on the way to Dewsbury in 1973, on 30 September, our coach caught fire and we had to bail out and get lifts. It was lucky the wind was blowing in the opposite direction to where we were sat as it could have been very serious indeed.

That season we won the BBC2 Floodlit Trophy by beating Dewsbury 22–2 in December, then we beat Widnes in the Challenge Cup and finally turned over Salford 15–2 for the Premiership. Even though we were successful, no one expected us to do anything. We beat Keighley in the Challenge Cup semi final by a point and still people doubted us. People forgot we had a team of good players. We were a difficult team to play against and when we were in the mood, almost impossible to beat. We beat Widnes in the Challenge Cup Final in 100 degrees heat, and then they said we wouldn't beat Salford the following week and we did. We could only win games after all and do no more, but it is fair to say we were motivated to beat these teams.

What set that particular team apart? I don't know, we just clicked. We did a lot of one to one tackling, unlike these days when the fad seems to be to get as many people in the tackle as possible. We ran in hard to get them to three-man tackle us and then used the space with a quick play the ball to create chances. Our gameplan was to take our plunges and use the gaps created. If you take three players into the tackle then there are two gaps to utilise. Maybe we weren't as confident the year before or perhaps our teammates couldn't make those tackles. Players picked their man and if the ball went somewhere else then it was someone else's problem.

That season people didn't score a lot against us. The likes of Mantle and co had engines that could go all day. Even though we won at Keighley 5–4, we spent the game in their half and felt comfortable. Provided they stayed in their half, we knew they wouldn't score. We soaked up the pressure and then got stuck into them in the second half. We had the most amazing self belief that we could hold them in the first half and then score points in the second.

That happened when we played Widnes at Wembley in the Challenge Cup Final. A great deal of the build up focussed on the fact we were an aging team and no one gave us a chance. The press said we were 'Dad's Army' and Murphy said he would jump off Runcorn Bridge if Widnes lost. We never spoke about those comments—preferring to concentrate on our own strengths and game, yet deep down these comments served to gee us all up. Before the game, I went down to London with

Widnes' Reggie Bowden to do a press conference and we had a few beers on the way back. We ended up in a bingo hall in Frodsham, drinking until we couldn't speak!

People lost sight of the fact that we were a good side because of the average age of our team. We may not have had the legs, but Mantle, Cunningham, Noonan and Mathias didn't become bad players overnight because they were older. They might lose a yard of pace, but they were capable of winning big matches. I don't think people respected that. We had been winning games all season so why would we suddenly fall down at the end? Widnes weren't a side that were often beaten by 20 points.

Our fans thought we would win and we made sure we were as focussed as possible in the build up. In 1972, we had a lot of injuries but this time around we knew who was playing. We announced the team early and the players were Geoff Pimblett; Les Jones, Eddie Cunningham, Derek Noonan, Roy Mathias; Billy Benyon, Geoff Heaton; John Mantle, Tony Karalius, Kel Coslett, Eric Chisnall, Georgie Nicholls, David Hull. Subs: Peter Glynn, Mel James. Our only disappointment was Frankie Wilson, who couldn't play. He thought he was fit and we didn't, so Eric called Benyon, Nichols, Pimblett and me into a meeting and asked if he should go on the bench. I said he shouldn't. Eventually Eric agreed so we went with Peter Glynn and he scored two tries. If Frankie had given his all in training then perhaps the decision would have been harder to make. I didn't think his injury allowed him to go flat out and he held back a little thinking he would be all right on the day.

We travelled down a couple of days early, after a day out in Blackpool, and stayed in Sevenoaks. It was a perfect setting. We sat in the garden of the hotel before the game looking at the surroundings and the last thing we thought about was the rugby match we were due to play in a few hours time. The drive into

Wembley was superb and most of the lads had their heads pressed up against the window watching the fans cheering us on. Once in the dressing room, we were in game mode. Ash talked about what was expected, mentioned Dad's Army and said they had a young front row. We wanted to bring them inside so we could put them in a pen, tackle them and exploit the gaps.

Even being there in 1972 didn't prepare us for how loud it was when we entered the field. It was 100 degrees out there and that heat hit us straightaway. The game was a real battle and a lot closer than the eventual scoreline suggested. Widnes had us on the rack for a long time and just before half time it was tight at 6–4. As the seconds ticked down, they did this move and Geoff Heaton tackled Dougie Laughton on the last. It was a ball we needed to win from the scrum, as they would have all the pressure on the stroke of half time if they won it. Thankfully, we fought for the ball, I fell on it and the whistle went. At half time we all had a big drink of water and oranges, and then went back out.

In the second half we took lots of pressure and camped in our own half. Then on 60 minutes, and still in our own half, Elwell from Widnes dropped a goal to make it 6–5. That took all the pressure off us. We were getting dehydrated and had done a lot of tackling in their half. From there, it was a case of keeping them out. But we came off our own line and Les Jones, and then Peter Glynn came on and scored two tries. Their decision to drop a goal to make it 6–5 was a big call for us as it meant the next scorer won the game. It was a tremendous battle and the scoreline doesn't represent the true picture. But we held out and I walked up the steps once more to receive the trophy, milked it for all its worth and Maggie Thatcher presented me with the cup. Dad's Army indeed…

If you look at pictures of me after the game I look totally

wrecked. And I was. It was 100 degrees and I jumped straight in the bath afterwards. I had smelling salts, the works, but it was no good. I was dehydrated and feeling lousy with a pounding head. When I got back to the hotel, our Director John Clegg banned me from drinking, told me to have a cold bath and drink lots of water. I recovered by 10 p.m. and then had my first pint. Staying sober until then seemed like a long three hours, I can tell you. After a couple of beers, I was tired and needed to go to bed.

After the usual reception at St Helens, we had recovery time ready for the Premiership the week after against Salford. They won the league that year and were a good side. It was touch and go in that game, we were losing 1–0 at half time, and again people doubted us, but we came through and did the double. As a reward for winning the league the previous season, we faced Eastern Suburbs in the World Club Challenge. We played three matches against Queensland and Auckland. Geoff Pimblett said the guys had had enough by the third game and I suppose that was right. We waited five or six weeks before going and in that time, we trailed the cups around working men's clubs and such to show them off. Also we trained, rather than played, and that took the shine off things, especially for players like us who were slightly past it.

We were in with a shout, but we needed to keep playing all the way up to the finals. To lose on tour isn't much fun. If we could have won one, then it wouldn't have been a bad tour. A few players were retiring and that was difficult. Despite losing all three games we had a good time, put the effort in and believed we could win them. It was an experience…and it was worthwhile taking the gamble and going out there.

One of the honours I had as Saints captain was to visit Buckingham Palace with Jacqueline for a special garden party. I was representing the town because we had won everything in

1976 and I had to take the Challenge Cup down with me as well. The garden party was part of the Queen's Jubilee and it was a tremendous experience. We stayed in Slone Street in the capital and walked down to the Palace. We actually went in the back entrance, which the guards thought was very amusing, but it was a fantastic day. I don't remember meeting the Queen though...

As for me? I had no regrets in retiring as I'd simply had enough with playing and training. I hung up my boots and decided to see what the real world could offer me.

15

'BUT MY RECORD STANDS AT 12 WINS FROM 17 MATCHES...'

I hadn't given coaching a second thought and wasn't particularly interested in continuing with the game because I felt I had done my time successfully. When Eric asked me to be his assistant at Saints I thought it was worth a punt. I began in the position on 21 August—unpaid of course—with the idea of just watching Ash in action and learning from him. And guess what? On my second day in the seat, the lads went on strike. They earned £40 for an away win, £30 for a home win and £15 for a loss. The club offered them an increase of a fiver a week but Geoff, as captain, said they wanted an extra £2 on top. I read recently that one of the lads told *The Sunday Times* that the only perk for winning at Wembley was a 'sweater and a bag'. Geoff himself said the money they made wasn't enough to keep the kids in toffees.

In my opinion they were talking about 1976 after it had gone. They should have sorted out the issue before the season began. The agreement was that the 1976 Challenge Cup winners' money should be shared out among the players. That's what was agreed. I'm not saying they were wrong, but I understood why they were annoyed. They probably didn't need to go on strike and could have made their case in other ways. In the end they allowed an 'A' Team to go to Wigan in the Lancashire Cup and Green Vigo ripped us apart. The players lost a wage through doing that and they could have met the Board afterwards. Vigo got seven tries that day.

I stayed at Saints until 15 November, joining Rochdale a day later as player-coach. I was happy to be an assistant and didn't retire from playing at the club with a playing-coach job, or any job as such, in mind. The player-coach position came about when I was away in France with Saints. I took a call from Jack Grindod asking if I was interested. I hadn't given it a thought to be honest. We arranged to meet and he put some suggestions to me which sounded alright. I was under no pressure to play and could play whenever it suited me. The offer was good and I accepted it.

After I told the club, Chairman Joe Seddon came to see me and said if I was going to play for them, then I could still play for the Saints. I said Rochdale had offered me a deal and I had virtually given my word. Saints couldn't match my offer and I didn't want to haggle anyway, so I followed it through.

Eric wasn't happy that I was leaving. It wasn't because of the decision I had made, but because the club decided to let me go without getting someone else in place. No finances were involved; pay was trivial and it was daft for me not to look at the terms that Rochdale were offering. That effected my decision of course. I had learnt a lot from Eric both from being a captain under him and from seeing his man management skills. I learnt not to bottle things up, and to get second opinions as I discovered this creates more choices. You don't have to listen to the opinions, but it is good to take them on board.

I had no real thoughts of taking a player-coach position. All I knew was that I was going to retire. I had a job repping for Kerr's and later at Whitbread and my wife went back to work as a private secretary so I was never concerned about a future career. I didn't need to carry on playing.

When I arrived at Rochdale, they had won one game in 12. That's why they needed help and I wanted to do my best for the club. I knew the job was going to be difficult but I took on the challenge. I have never been frightened of a challenge—I showed that when I signed for Saints and when I went from Llanelli to Aberavon.

I brought a couple of players into Rochdale and we ended up being a decent team. Geoff Heaton—my teammate at Saints was a fantastic player in the side and gave it some organisation. He led from the front and was a significant factor in the team that gained promotion. One of the problems with Rochdale was its geography. Travelling to Rochdale was a pain and so if someone came in with an offer for a player that the club accepted, the vast majority of the time the player wanted to leave. That meant we never really had a settled side. That was a shame. I created a decent side to find it dismantled as quickly as I had put it together. Players were noticed playing for the club and got picked off easily. When we got into the first division, the likes of Charlie Birdsall went to Hull, Wally Jones went to Warrington, Ashcroft went to Swinton and the team disappeared. We were a decent side until we started selling and that didn't work for me.

In our first season, 1976–77, we were unlucky to go down. We finished 13th with 22 points from 30 games. We won 10 of the last 18 games in effect and still went down. It was unlucky I suppose as the damage occurred earlier in the year. I didn't mind playing and coaching. As captain of a team, you coach on the field and Peter Gartlan did a good job as my assistant. The lads knew their position and what they had to do. We did well to beat Saints, Leeds and Hull KR. Ken Kelly came out of retirement to play for us and then Alex Murphy signed him for Warrington.

We only trained twice a week, sometimes at weekends. They all knew the rules and turned up as they knew that if they didn't turn up for training, then they wouldn't play. Whether you were an international or not, these were the rules and everyone knew them. On Boxing Day Alan Rathbone missed out, as he hadn't turned up for training. We were a disciplined club and when you think of the players we had, that was a real achievement.

Putting your stamp on a team comes with training, but when someone breaks the rules then you can enforce them and show how strong a coach you can be. We played as a team and everyone pitched in together. Winning helped our spirits and we became confident.

When I came in to Rochdale, I had to look at the defence as we were losing games we should have won. I always believed that teams should stop the opposition scoring and make them work for their points. The players that came in were capable of tackling. We couldn't compete with teams like Saints and Leeds in terms of points scoring, but we could contain them just by keeping them out. We were never going to beat Saints by 30 points, therefore we had to limit their chances. And that's what we did. The players did well and put themselves in the shop window. If they could play well for us, they could play well for anyone and the lads saw that. We won at Widnes when they were in their pomp. Teams gave us some respect and that was a real feel good factor at the club.

No opposition wanted to come to Rochdale. It was always cold and one night we played Wigan in the BBC2 Floodlit Trophy. The game was called off on the Tuesday night so we played a day later. Let's be honest, conditions wouldn't exactly have improved. My team talk was simply this. 'Who the bloody hell wants to come here when it's pouring with rain? They don't want to come here…let's welcome them with open arms and stick them in the mud.'

We beat them. It was a case of mind over matter! They didn't want to be here, so we didn't disappoint them! That's how we overcame teams like that—through not welcoming them and keeping them in their place. I came off that night after playing in the first half. It was so cold I couldn't give a team talk. I jumped in the bath, boots and everything, and told Peter to get Alan Bailey on and get them back out. I played against the wind and rain and felt I had done my whack!

We were promoted the year after only to be relegated again the year after that. I enjoyed my time there. The people were nice; I went to the ground, played and went home. I enjoyed the welcome and the Board were great. Success was our only downfall and when teams saw how well players could compete at 'lowly' Rochdale, the side broke up. After a while I realised there was no future. We had no team, we were losing and I told Jack I couldn't be arsed! I was out of the game and probably a little happier for it. Then, in December 1979, Wigan approached me to be their new coach.

Similar to when I joined Rochdale, when I joined Wigan they were in a bit of a state. They had played 11 matches and had just one point. A total of 17 games later, they had 25 points. We won 12 out of 17 games, and let's be honest, that's not bad considering the state they were in. Of course the record books show Wigan were relegated fourth from bottom that season and my name will ever be alongside that statistic. But my record of 12 wins from 17 matches stands, especially as I had a team with only one point when I joined.

I had no reservations about joining Wigan considering I'd been at Rochdale and then out of the game. It didn't cross my mind that I was a Saints lad. It's a game of rugby after all. On arriving at Central Park, I was very disappointed with Wigan. There was either no discipline, or they were trying it on with me, I don't know. Training was at half six, a few times a week and players turned up 10 and 20 minutes late. I was surprised.

But it didn't take long to turn around this attitude, and they started to believe in themselves. The team weren't as good as Wigan of old, but once they realised everyone was in the same boat, they gave their all. The team that went down was the team that started the season. We didn't buy anyone and they really gave it a go. We might have lost a cup tie, but winning 12 from 17 games wasn't bad. It wasn't exactly a poor side.

The players were great with me but Green Vigo didn't play after I suspended him for going drinking before a cup game. I took the players to Holland Hall Hotel after training to tell them how important the cup game was against Hull KR. I told them not to drink and not only did he drink, but he went to the Riverside nightclub and drank there too. I confronted him and he said he only had a few beers, so I dropped him for a couple of games. He walked out and never came back. He knew the rules and that was that as far as I was concerned.

George Fairburn was captain, played his heart out and became coach after me. Once the local boys such as Denis Boyd understood the rules they gave it their all and they deserved to stay in the First Division. In our last game away at Castleford, we just weren't good enough and we went down. Now I was back in the game, Saints were sniffing around and I told the Wigan Chairman, Harry Costello, that they had approached me. I think he just accepted that I planned to leave. Or maybe he thought I hadn't done a good job, I don't know. I would have stayed if I'd had the opportunity. Joining Saints was never an option as the foundations were laid at Wigan for me to continue my good work for another year at least. I still believe we could have moved forward from there. I did a good job for them with tremendous help from my number two Wilf Smith, put the ship back in the water and sailed it straight. I was disappointed with their attitude and especially with Harry's attitude. He assumed I was going to Saints.

Of course I take a lot of stick for taking Wigan down, because of who I am. Sometimes I find myself giving reasons. They did all right for me and in black and white that record speaks for itself. Anyone else who thinks I didn't do a good job should sit down and read the statistics.

When I headed to Saints the following year (1980–81), they were also struggling at the wrong end of the table. I went in and did well to get them to eighth and also to make the semi final of the Challenge Cup. It was a real feather in my cap as we weren't a good side. Once you start to win, people want you to win more.

In the game over the last few years, many underhand things have been done to coaches behind closed doors, whether it be clandestine meetings or talking behind their backs. What happened to me must have happened to a lot of other people. I fell out with a few of the Saints Directors and some of them took their ball home if they didn't get their own way.

The only player I ever wanted at Wigan was Trevor Skerritt. He was on the transfer list for £30k, played for Wales and was a good player before he made his name. The Wigan Board decided to sign a chap from Featherstone instead and he only ever played twice for the 'A' Team. Trevor went to Hull for 40k in the end and the rest is history.

Saints needed players too. I bought Gary Moorby from Keighley and he scored 25 tries for me. I also wanted Paul Grimes from Leigh—he was a prop listed for £3k. The Board denied this request. Billy Benyon eventually paid £30k for Paul from Whitehaven. He was a prop and would have been great for me.

As I've said, Saints weren't a great team when I joined them and certainly not a top of the table team like they are now. Barry Ledger and Neil Holding were all coming through but the likes of Nicholls and Chisnall were there. They were getting past it and should have been spoken to about retiring a couple of years before I came. I took the captaincy off George Nicholls as I thought he was past it and far too influential. He wanted to be the ball handler and the playmaker. He was a good rugby league forward and I think he thought with the captaincy came ball handling. It was up to me to try to explain that his position in the game had changed. That was a difficult conversation, but he took it in good spirit. In the end, I gave the captaincy to Eric Chisnall.

In hindsight, taking the captaincy off Nicholls wasn't wrong but I should have given it to Harry Pinner. He was a young man and my decision was the wrong one. Harry was buzzing. Although he had his faults I think he would have been ideal as well as being someone for the rest of the team to look up to. Captaining your club is an honour and getting it right for all parties is a real balancing act. It is a damn sight easier to do these things when you are winning. But when you are losing, as we were, it makes it all the more difficult.

As Chisnall was captain, I probably expected a little more from him. We were always struggling for props so I asked him to play prop forward to help the team. I picked him at prop for our home match against Whitehaven, pinned up the team sheet, he looked at it and said he wasn't playing.

In those days coaches presented their team to the Board a couple of days before the game and understandably Tom Ashcroft, Chairman, and Director Joe Pickavance asked me why Eric wasn't playing. I said he didn't want to play prop and I would play Tony Bolton at eight instead. Joe wanted to hear it from the horse's mouth so Tom and I drove to Eric's house and had a chat. It was all very civil, we had a brew and Eric said he didn't want to play at 'eight' and that was it. He had played there a couple of times during the season.

When I came into the club on match day Eric was walking out of the dressing room. We had a chat and he said he was not playing at number eight. I said: 'Well that's fine. You're not playing.' Later, Tony Bolton was getting ready for the game and just tying his boots when Ashcroft came in and told me he'd had a chat with Eric and Eric had decided he would play at prop. I looked at him and said: 'He won't. There is a fella here changed and ready to go.' Eric didn't stay at the club long after that and went to Leigh. As a prop forward.

I always played in a position that was best for the team, not for me. It was the same when I decided not to kick goals—it was always for the team. There were no glory boys and that is what I wanted. Rightly or wrongly, my decision over Eric upset a few people and I suppose from that point I was always on my way out. A few of the Directors in that room weren't happy with my decision and it was the beginning of the end for me at the club. It's easy for Directors to be coaches from their offices!

After that incident we still had a few games to play and we went on to win most of them. Everyone knew the score and that they were playing for St Helens. We wanted the people of the town to be proud of us. But at the end of the 1982 season the Board didn't renew my contract. When I came to Saints I knew the existing coach, Eric Ashton, was happy, as he knew I was coming and he was moving on to the Board. But when the Board approached a replacement a coach, I knew I was up the swanny! They ended up with Billy Benyon although he wasn't their first choice. I know they also approached Ray French and another player too.

Perhaps I should have had another year at Saints. We won the majority of our remaining nine games so something was going right. If the following season had gone poorly, I would have left at the end of the year anyway, but at least the choice would have been mine to make. Saints weren't a top team, yet they did well in my final season.

Perhaps my decision about Chissy made the Board think I was working against them. I remember once we were travelling up to Barrow by coach. The Directors sat in the front of the coach, I was in the middle and the players were at the back. The Board were playing cards and were one short, so I stepped in. We played Napoleon, and I won £20. Some of the Board stopped playing when we hit Charnock Richard as they thought I was cheating. I gave my winnings to Chissy to get the lads a few beers anyway.

All things being said, I enjoyed my involvement at Saints. Losing to Hull KR in the Challenge Cup semi final was hard. It was five all at half time and they killed us in the second half. Afterwards I came into the players' lounge and no one talked to me apart from Sam Hall, one of the Directors. I was disappointed too. It mattered to me back then when they lost just as much as it pains me now.

Coaching is a strange business. One day you are up, one day you are down. You win, lose and most coaches live and breathe for their job. My wife Jacqueline saw it coming though. Colleagues who were her friends abused her and blanked her when we lost. She took more flack than me. Perhaps I didn't hear the flack, or was good at letting it go. She didn't enjoy that time whereas I thought it was the norm!

16

'BEING OUT OF THE GAME TOOK A BIT OF ADJUSTMENT...'

I have never really been the sort of person to bear a grudge or be bitter. Throughout this book I have remembered things and might come across as a little upset by them. If I sound bitter as a result, then forgive me. Being out of the game took a bit of adjustment but I was never one to dwell on what might have been. I was just very disappointed with the way I was let go.

People win and lose, and I just thought an extra 12 months was all I could have asked for. If things hadn't gone my way for that extra season then I would have left of my own accord anyway. Three years at a club is long enough to turn things around, get established and build a core base of players. My anger stems from not being given that time, because towards the end of the season at Saints, there was light at the end of the tunnel.

During the time I was at Knowsley Road, I bought one player from Keighley and he scored a bundle of tries. The club always said they had no money, but he was the only one they bought anyway. That one worked out all right. Ironically, when my contract wasn't renewed they signed Paul Grimes who I had been pushing them to sign for months previously. It seemed like the things I suggested weren't good enough whilst I was there but when I left, they were only too pleased to make them happen.

I was never worried about not working. When I coached I worked at Kerr's Minerals, run by a club Director. To save both our embarrassment, I changed companies and it was a great move for me. I went from a local brand to an established worldwide brewery firm in Whitbread. It did me a lot of good.

Being out of the game did not worry me at all, although I felt like I still had a lot to put back in. I picked up some sponsorship work and became involved in the big Rugby League Cup ties and games so I still saw people. Doing little things like that around the game kept me happy. Being out of the public eye never worried me either. Some players disappear from the limelight because they go into a job where they can be a 'normal' member of the public. Ex-players like Paul Sculthorpe are picked up by the media and become the face of a club, because they had bloody good careers. Scully will notice a difference as time goes on of course, but for the time being he will find that the good things he did will stand him in good stead in the future. His name will get him in places, open doors, but whether he clinches the deal will be up to him.

I was lucky to be a rep for such a good company as Whitbread. I faced the public with the reputation of an ex-player and coach. I also had the advantage that meeting people in pubs and clubs was something I had done all my life. I didn't have a job where I went into a room and saw no one. I was out and about and being an ex-player certainly helped me. Both things went hand in glove really. The job was all about mixing with the public so I couldn't stay in and feel sorry for myself. Instead of having two jobs, now I had the one and I had to get on and do it.

Whitbread didn't have much business in St Helens when I

started and I managed to build up a good patch. I enjoyed talking to the stewards and landlords in the free trade part of the business, and that was where my interest in horse racing escalated. Whitbread produced Trophy Bitter and, fortunately for me, they sponsored the Great Britain Rugby League team for three seasons. This enabled me to attend the internationals with customers and it was a real pleasure. I had many happy trips with my sales teammates and customers and made some good friends. One memorable trip took us to a beer festival in Germany and we went on a boat trip. Unfortunately, on the return journey, we got on the boat heading the wrong way and were duly turfed off further down the river. This meant we had to find our way back to the hotel on a bus. One of my colleagues, Alistair Patterson, who was a vicar's son, proceeded to hum the tune from the film *The Great Escape* all the way back to the bus—we got some strange looks from the other passengers!

Another time the Liverpool team won a national Whitbread contest for selling the most Heineken. The prize was three days on the QEII. It was a great trip. We travelled to Southampton by coach and sailed to the Channel Isles and then Ireland before returning to Liverpool. It was something I would never have done if I hadn't worked for Whitbread. I enjoyed working for a company that allowed me to get involved in rugby league and mix with lots of people. It was great to be a part of something and attending those internationals were special occasions too.

Jacqueline was upset I lost the coaching job but it worked out in the end. I didn't have much of a home life holding down two jobs so at least I was home more! And she didn't have to take abuse anymore either. It is wrong to say that we were all glad it happened as we spent more time at home, but we accepted it, overcame it and enjoyed our time together. My kids were teenagers so it certainly took a bit of time to get to know them again too!

She was glad it worked out in the end as she was witness to the back stabbing that coaches get. She had seen it in my playing days but she saw more of it when I was a coach. There always seemed to be someone complaining. I think deep down she was probably pleased that I was doing more of a 'nine to five' job. When I was playing I was always on the go. When I finished playing I still did a bit of training down at UGB in St Helens, throwing the ball around and keeping myself going with the amateur lads down there. But it drifted away from me as I got older. I wasn't a fitness fanatic but I liked to keep myself going.

When I was repping, I came back into the game as the Welsh manager. I was delighted to be offered the position and really enjoyed it. It was just a shame that, like now, we don't have enough players to keep on going. I was manager for a couple of seasons with coach Neil Kelly, but after a while we didn't have the players and therefore didn't have a team. I know we didn't qualify for the World Cup in 2008 but hopefully with Crusaders in Super League they will regularly have enough players for the Welsh team and qualify for the next World Cup. It would be good if they could get a few local lads at the Crusaders as that could mean the start of something big for the national team. I was also approached by Dougie Laughton who asked me to go and help Jon Davies at Widnes as well as Graham Oldroyd and Francis Cummins at Leeds as their goal kicking coach. I am forever grateful for that as it kept me further involved in the game. I was also very proud that he had chosen me.

There are some feeder teams in Wales and there are enough players to dig out. League is a good game to play in if you want to be involved with the ball. I maintain the players are there but Celtic and Wales need time to get people to play so they can see what a good game it is. Young players might also see that they can make a few bob in the League too and that rugby league might provide a future for them.

At about this time, Silk Cut were sponsoring the Rugby League Challenge Cup at Wembley and they hired a PR firm called Karen Earle to run this for them. Karen Earle contacted the rugby league HQ and asked for the names of two ex players to work with them. My name and Clive Sullivan's name were put forward and we started to attend matches, look after the press and check the advertising hoardings were in the right place. Unfortunately, soon after this started, Clive became ill and died. He had cancer. His early death was very sad; he was such a great ambassador for the game of rugby league. Despite Clive's death, it was an enjoyable time for me and I enjoyed visiting all the clubs again that I had played against in the past. I was pleasantly surprised with the reception I received at these clubs and people could not have done more to help or make me welcome. It gave me a real boost.

I had spent 16 years in and out of the game when I was asked to return to Saints on the marketing side in 1998. At that time, Whitbread had been evaluating its market standing and decided to show the door to anyone in their mid fifties. So as well as getting a decent package and all that comes with it, I also got an opportunity to the test the selling skills I had learnt outside the club.

Returning to Saints was an easy decision to make. It was my club for a start. I had played and coached there and felt like I knew the people who worked behind the scenes. And it looked exactly the same as when I first played there so many years ago! It was the reason I left Wales and returning to my base was absolutely brilliant. I hoped the selling skills I'd developed at Whitbread could be adapted for the marketing side of rugby league and I was looking forward to seeing how much the game had developed since I'd left.

When I came into the game back in 1962, sponsorship wasn't a big part of it. There was the odd firm or local club that would throw some money in but nothing like the levels you see today. These days, clubs can't live without sponsorship. One of my special deals was to bring Pilkington back on board. They were the town's main employer and weren't involved in the game or in sponsoring the Saints at the time. Pilks and Saints went hand in hand when I played for Saints. Lord and Lady Pilkington were involved in everything and you couldn't have a dinner without inviting them. Lord and Lady Pilkington often invited players to Windle Hall for dinners. I found it strange that they didn't have any sort of involvement in the club anymore.

My colleague Andy Foreman and I arranged a meeting with Ste Gange at the glassmaker and asked if they would sponsor Saints. Credit to Ste, he worked hard and came back with some funding. In 2009 they were Saints' title sponsor as they realised what a massive brand Saints had become. These days Pilkingtons may be a multinational firm with plants all round the world, but it will always be a St Helens company. It is a company that, in my opinion, should be associated with the town's other great product—trophy winning rugby league.

Going back to my Whitbread days, I enjoyed making the deals and was naturally disappointed when I couldn't seal one. Pilkington had drifted away from the club and I was glad that Andy and I got them to dip their toes in rugby league once more. The two were together once again as they should be.

I came back to the club at the time of Super League in 1996. It heralded a new era, but I thought it was pretty much the same league in all but name. Of course, we were playing in summer, but it didn't make it a superior game because it was called Super League. In effect, the game was sold for TV and a major step forward for all involved.

Playing wise, there were 'ability' players in my day too. Players will always come through if they are good enough and changing the title of the league doesn't suddenly mean all those players will come through. Moving the season to summer meant the tracks were drier, harder and the game got faster. There will always be arguments about who is good, and who is not as good but the game is still rugby league whatever the rules.

Super League seemed to be the catalyst for St Helens to kick on. The club created a carnival atmosphere around summer rugby and its academy system meant younger players could come through. Of course, some of the league's other teams brought in overseas players to improve their teams. In my view, you should only sign players from overseas if they are better than those you have already. If you are signing players just to fill gaps then that does nothing for the competition. So the players you do sign have to be able to improve the competition and be a beacon for the younger players to aspire to.

To get a Visa in my day, a player had to be exceptional, and rightly so. In my subsequent role as the club's Football Manager, I used to call immigration to see what I could do to help bring the Visa process forward. That interaction was important to me and the club as I became familiar with the people at immigration and vice versa. When the likes of Darren Albert and Jamie Lyon came in I, explained to the officials how important they would be to the club. I tried to show they were important players so hopefully they would hurry the process if at all possible.

If an overseas player is a benefit to the game, then that is key. That's why there needs to be a strict quota. I don't disagree with overseas players coming in but a mediocre player that does nothing for the game is not what we need. It's all about adding value to the competition and encouraging the locals to play.

That's what will be happening at Celtic.

I took over from Eric Hughes towards the end of the millennium as the club's Football Manager. Eric was much-vilified by the fans because of what happened with Ellery Hanley and it is not my place to comment on that. He got on well with me. I thought he was a top man and there was no harm in him at all. Before he left, he let me work with him for a month to ease me into the job.

Being a football manager was fun. It reminded me of why I wanted another year as coach back in 1982, mainly because I understood more of what went on behind the scenes at a rugby league club. Back in my last year of coaching, I felt I had ironed out the squad and that the team was relatively settled. Some players were in the twilight of their careers and as a player it is always difficult to know when it is the right time to finish. They need to decide whether to keep playing, move on, go into coaching or whatever. This also happened at Wigan in the seventies with Brian McTigue and co. A club needs to be strong in moving players on if they are too old, or not right, and then bring the youngsters through. I felt we had done that at Saints, and getting to the semi final of the Challenge Cup may have papered over the cracks, but shows that Saints had potential. That's why I wanted another season.

To be a Saints player, you need to be good. Then, you need to perform week in week out. One good performance a month doesn't make you a Saints player. In 1982, there was no money to buy players and the Board had different opinions. When there are 12 people together, it is impossible to please them all the time. As a coach, you can only do what you think is right for the club. You want to do the best that you can. Obviously people have little patience, they want things to happen tomorrow and getting that blend is very difficult. When I left Saints they won a couple of trophies. Now, I'm not saying it was my team, but I laid the foundations of it. Couldn't I have taken them to that silverware?

Working behind the scenes meant I got to know more about people's opinions. Currently, I am the club's gameday manager. I enjoy what I am doing because I am part of it, but without any authority or the resultant pressure. My job is to help on match day and to make things easier for players and staff and whoever else needs me. If we have any obstacles, I will take them away. I'm just a helper really, rather than a coaching figure. I suggest to players what needs to be done off the field rather than on it and if any of the staff on match day have an issue, I will go beyond myself to sort it out.

That's not to say I don't have opinions, it can be difficult not to coach at times—especially when I first took on the role. What I have tried to do is to keep my opinions to myself, but I will give my view when, and if, I am asked. I don't tell people what they should or shouldn't do as that's no longer my job. I just admire what goes on unless someone asks me what I think. I just enjoy the camaraderie and let the coaching staff do their jobs. I am here to help it they want to talk to me.

I believe that people need to talk. If someone wants to ask me something it's not a problem. If they don't want to ask me something, that's not a problem either. I get to see what goes on behind closed doors and I really enjoy it as it keeps me going. As a fullback and loose forward, it can be difficult to watch players in these positions, but again, it isn't my position to say what they are doing right or wrong. Recently I was chatting with Saints' scrum half, Sean Long, when we were in the stands together watching a game. I enjoyed the game and we were both embroiled in why a certain player did this or that.

I do believe the game is coached too much off the field and I feel players could think more for themselves. It isn't a criticism, just the structure and the plans they work under these days. No one seems to take the game by the scruff of the neck without listening to the coach first.

Anyway, back to the game day. Match day is a finely tuned operation and I am there to help when something goes wrong. We ran out of water before we faced Catalans in Perpignan and I went on a run to a French Hypermarket to find some. That incident is a precise illustration of my role. At away games I do whatever the team needs me to do. On match day there are a lot of little things I have to do but the players are brought up into it and kind of fall into it anyway through experience.

Daniel Anderson liked to talk to the Match Commissioner at games. He always had a question, whether it was about the colours of jerseys or something concerning the rules. We played at Wakefield once and, along with the rest of the coaching staff, we sat in the boxes behind the goals at Belle Vue. Daniel told me he wanted to speak to the Commissioner about some issue he had so I had to leave the boxes, go to the half way line, get through the crowd and go up the stairs to find him. Then the Commissioner told me he couldn't talk to him until after the game. So I had to go all the way back…and I'm not a young man these days either. But that's what I am there for.

Of course, there's some more pleasurable parts to the role. I organise a few beers on the coach if we win a cup tie and sort out accreditation for Cup Finals and so on. I just ensure things go smoothly. I have paraded around Wembley with the players and been on open top bus tours. We used to do open top bus tours all the time but stopped in the late nineties as the club preferred to get the lads and the crowds back to the stadium. The return to the open top bus tour in 2007 was superb. We took the club back to the people. It's easy to condemn the exercise as a waste of time but on the route were elderly people, disabled people, as well as kids and other people just making the effort to see the Saints with the cup. It was a way of thanking the supporters and was an absolutely tremendous thing to do.

The open top bus tour in 2007 was also memorable for two other things. The first thing was that they forgot to schedule a toilet break into the tour. I'm sure you can imagine the mess there would have been if there had been no toilet break at all. The lads had had a few beers and part way into the tour, I suddenly realised they might need a break, so we hurriedly pulled into the stadium! My sudden realisation was actually down to insider information when I remembered what it was like when I played! Then, about a mile into the tour, the top of the bus got caught in some sagging bunting. The resultant ducking by the players and staff was more than justified when a black drainpipe flew in the bus with the bunting. I have no idea whose head the bunting got tangled up in first. Although it was funny at the time, it could have been quite serious I suppose. Then in 2008 when we passed the same spot again after winning the Challenge Cup for the third time, we saw a few tipsy supporters parading that same broken bit of drainpipe.

The game has given me an education and the confidence to get on in life. It is the reason I left home and has kept me going over the years. It has been great for me. I was lucky enough to play for a long time, to coach and then to be employed behind the scenes as well. It has kept me involved with people and I don't think there is a better education than being with people.

17

'HERE'S MY DREAM TEAM...'

I have played with many players over the years so selecting my best 13 (and four subs) from all those countless faces is easily the hardest thing I have had to do in the course of writing this book.

Do I go for a hybrid team made up of union or league players or do I pick a side from each? These were all questions I had to answer when creating my Dream Team. In the end, I went for a rugby league team, as I spent most of my career in the game, and then suggested a few 'Unionites' who would be best placed to fill in if we needed them.

I would be happy to play anyone with this team and the most difficult thing has been deciding who to leave out. I could have picked another two or three teams without question or hesitation.

But at the time of speaking, this would be the side I would choose. In every position, I could have picked another four or five players. Please note that I am not calling the players I have omitted, this is only my opinion at the end of the day!

I hope my XIII (plus four) will enjoy playing together. Incidentally, I have picked them in positions suited to my team to ensure real balance to take on all comers!

1. Geoff Pimblett (St Helens 1970–78)

It was a real dilemma as to whether to choose Geoff Pimblett or Frankie Barrow. This spot could only be filled by one of these two guys really. When I broke my leg, Frankie came into the team to cover for me and did a great job. He was a defensive fullback who you could always count on if someone broke through.

After all our successful years in the seventies, Geoff just edges it. He was a centre/stand off when he signed, but he had tremendous tackling and attacking ability. So for the balance of the team, he gets the vote. He had that extra dimension, could read the play really well and he could defend when called upon. Defence wasn't perhaps his strongest point, but with the other players in front of him, it was a very rare event indeed if he was asked to be our last line of defence. For his attacking ability alone, he gets the vote.

2. Tom Van Vollenhoven (St Helens 1957–67)

This is clearly the most obvious choice of the whole XIII. When I came to Saints, Tom was everything people talked about. I played behind him at fullback and then up front as loose forward. Quite simply, he was a tremendous winger in both attack and defence. He was a great team man as well with a very dry sense of humour. He was probably, when you compare him with Billy Boston and Brian Bevan, the complete winger.

3. Billy Benyon (St Helens 1961–77)

Billy was a good centre and footballer who could handle the ball with the best of them. He also oozed quality in defence.

4. John Walsh (St Helens 1967–74)

John was a tremendous footballer whose versatility could see him play at stand off, fullback or centre. Like Billy, he had an excellent footballing brain. He never shirked anything. I would be happy to play against anyone with Billy and John in my team.

5. Roy Mathias (St Helens 1972–82)
It is difficult to pick two standout wingers for my team and that is why I have allowed myself some substitutes! Honest Roy had pace, strength and wouldn't shirk the hard work. He also had other facets to his game but I saw Roy as an attacking winger.

6. Frank Myler (St Helens 1967–70)
Frank may only have been at Saints for a few years, but his time was superb. It was an experience to play with him. His knowledge of the game was second to none and I was sad to see him leave.

7. Alex Murphy (St Helens 1955–65)
Again, this guy had some ability. Okay, he would take his ball home now and again, but in this team, he would be superb. Incidentally, both Frank and Alex were amazing half backs and both are in the record books. There's no problem with their ability and they would have led this team round the park.

I have been lucky to play with some superb forwards in my career and I could have chosen around three packs that would have given this side real go forward. Unfortunately I might have left out some people who may have expected to be in. I wouldn't want the other players to think: 'Bloody hell, he's left me out.' There are some great players I haven't included, but like a coach, I have to pick the right team, with the right balance at the right time. I have had a longer vision I suppose, so don't hold a gun to my head, this is my team and it includes the best players I have played with!

8. John Warlow (St Helens 1963–68/73–74)

John propped in rugby union so he was no mug. He could run, handle the ball well and had the ability and strength.

9. Bill Sayer (St Helens 1965–70)

Initially signed for a cup run, Bill ended up on the team for five years! He was an athlete, a footballer and excelled in the no tackle rule as he could go all day.

10. Cliff Watson (St Helens 1960–70)

Cliff was a mountain of a man, with speed, strength and real ability.

11. Dick Huddart (St Helens 1958–63)
12. John Mantle (St Helens 1964–75)

In Dick and John you had two runners and two tacklers. They ran all over the field and would do anything for you. It was a real privilege to play with these guys.

13. Kel Coslett (St Helens 1962–76)

I enjoyed loose forward and when I joined league, deep down I wanted to play loose forward. In school I played at stand off and also played there for my town team and the Welsh Schoolboys. I reverted to fullback from youth rugby as I was a biggish lad and it made sense for me to play there. I played at fullback for Bynea youth, Llanelli and Wales. I just related to that position because of my size.

I enjoyed fullback, but when circumstances changed after breaking my leg I had the opportunity to play loose forward and I grabbed that with both hands. I enjoyed playing there. I enjoyed the decision making, involvement and responsibility and the fact that you can dictate the game—much like I did at stand off during my schoolboy days.

My rugby league career was at loose forward really and I enjoyed rugby more in that position. I wouldn't want to go back to fullback, but did when it mattered, and had no problem with it. But I am a loose forward. As for Coslett, well, he gave his all! The point is I would play my part in a good side and playing with such quality wouldn't frighten me at all.

Each of the players I have listed have helped me in my career and this team would take on all comers. I would be captain too. I would have thought that's how it works. In that team there aren't many captains but Myler could be my vice captain. Alex Murphy could do it, but I have seen him stick his jersey up his arse and play because his teammates were doing better than him. But he gets in because he was a top player in a team of top players.

I would goal kick too with Walsh and Pimblett backing up if I had a bad day. I don't feel I can turn around after kicking my entire career and give the responsibility to John or Geoff. I didn't kick for the last few years of my playing career because I was doing other things and propping, but as it's my team and I chose it, then I'm the kicker. I let Geoff kick in those final years at Saints. If I wanted, I could have gone for more records by kicking for another couple of seasons.

Anyway, on to the substitutes. These guys could have been in the starting team and would come in without weakening the side at all.

14. Mick Sullivan (St Helens 1960–62)

Mick just pips Les Jones as he could have played centre or wing and appeared in the pack now and again too. He was also a quality defensive player.

15. Tommy Bishop (St Helens 1965–68)
On his day, Tommy was one of the best backs around.

16. George Nicholls (St Helens 1972–80)
George was a real workhorse with speed, ability and the knack to create something out of nothing.

17. Eric Chisnall (St Helens 1966–81)
Again, Eric was a real workhorse with all the ability and footballing nouse you needed.

I would go for Cliff Evans as Head Coach with Eric Ashton as his assistant. Both were rugby players with real qualities and footballing brains. Cliff had the vision of the game and the moves came from him. Both would listen to suggestions and they would do a great job with that time. With a 17 man squad of that calibre the game would benefit, unless the team won everything. That would spoil it! Of course, several rugby union players from my Llanelli, Aberavon and Wales days would fit in well to this team. Terry Davies could play at fullback. He was a village lad who played for Wales and the Lions and he put me on the right track. Carwyn James could be half back, Ken Thomas could be on the wings with John Collins (because he could play the piano). Peter Jones, Malcolm Price, Terry Price and Brian Butler could make it into this team too.

This side would have done well in any era. They all had the ability. Bill Sayer would run the ball and get around them; Mathias started the winger taking up the ball to relieve the pressure. Mantle would run into the centres to create the space and Watson got involved in the four man tackle to open up gaps when they got off him. He was like an ox and they couldn't stop him.

So who would we play against? These are probably the

best players I have faced:

1. **Dai Watkins (Salford)**

2. **Billy Boston (Wigan)**

3. **Eric Ashton (Wigan)**

4. **Neil Fox (Wakefield)**

5. **John Stopford (Wigan)**

6. **Alan Hardisty (Castleford/Leeds)**

7. **Keith Hepworth (Leeds)**

8. **Jim Mills (Widnes)**

9. **'Flash' Flannigan (Hull KR)**

10. **Bill Ramsay (Leeds)**

11. **Phil Lowe (Hull KR)**

12. **Brian McTigue (Wigan)**

13. **Dougie Laughton (Widnes)**

What a team that would be. We would play the game at either Headingley in Leeds or at Wigan's Central Park. Knowsley Road would be our training base. We played top games at these venues with the crowds packed in and effectively on top of the players. The first time I played at Central Park, I caught Dave Bolton with a shoulder and as I stood underneath the posts as they kicked the penalty, the fans gave it to me. I always knew when it was a big game, because the fans gave us some stick, like at Swansea when I booted the ball off the touchline. I felt wanted when I was being booed as then I knew it was a big game.

Of course, with these two teams, the game would be tight. Voll would torment them and we would try not to give Hardisty and Hepworth a sniff. We would win, by a point, with a Coslett penalty off the touchline, on half way, in the driving rain.

18

'MORE VARIETY PLEASE...'

Some people say the game of rugby league is a lot different to how it was in my day. Of course, the six tackle rule replaced the four tackle rule and then the unlimited tackle days and the game got quicker as a result. But I maintain that any of my 'dream team' would rip up the league these days. Rugby league is a simple game, and everyone is entitled to their opinion, but I wish the modern day player would show a little more invention on the field.

One of the things that particularly annoys me is when players opt to go for the try instead of kicking perfectly placed penalties. But how many times do these attempts succeed? In some games you need every point you can gather and players and teams rebuke simple, very kickable penalties. I'm sure if the world stopped for a second and players thought about it, they would take more shots at goal.

Whether that means doing more decision making off the field than on it, I don't know. I suppose some of the blame lies as much on the coaches who want to be the decision makers as it does with a lack of decision makers on the field. Perhaps the players are frightened of making the decision and choosing the logical choice when the opportunity arises. Players on most teams will 'lay' to the bench rather than making decisions themselves.

In my day, I could kick penalties from all over the field and it was an 'easy' two points. If the penalty was in the opposition's half, or even on the half way line, I would have a pop. I think there are those kinds of players in the league now, but most will opt to run for the try. You will never find out if you can make a kick unless you try will you? Whether this is down to the change of balls from leather, I don't know. Perhaps players just can't kick new balls as far. We started with leather balls that took all the rain and were like a bar of soap when they were wet. Then they moved to non-slippery leather but they both sailed when you whacked them with your boot. Whether you can't get the same distance with the new ball, I'm not sure.

I honestly think if you have a side with a kicker who can kick from the half way line, then it gives your team a real advantage. It also means that the opposition is very unlikely to make an indiscretion in their own half. Thus, you get space to play rugby in, as the opposition won't go offside as much. They can come offside more if you aren't going to punish them with points. And kicking two points can make all the difference.

And, how many times can you score when you opt to run the penalty? Sometimes it is worth it for the opposition to go offside then. If you had someone who could kick from your own half, then they would make sure they stayed onside and didn't pinch yardage. I know teams like Saints, Leeds and Wigan will always back themselves to score a try and who can blame them with the teams they have? But I think it gives extra pressure to the attacking side that perhaps they don't need to put on themselves.

In my day we wanted to score and wanted the opposition to tackle our big man as that left gaps around the field for our backs and wingers to exploit. That is now popular in the modern game—big props will have four or five men tackling them for six, 12 or 18 tackles and that means if you can play the ball quickly you can exploit the shortage of people on the flanks. That's why the wingmen of today have more walk-ins than ever before.

When we played, we had a defensive structure that meant one man tackled another. Obviously if they were in trouble we would double up, but the general rule was one man per tackle. Then, if the ball came out, another man would be ready to tackle him. That meant we were set up for anything else and the gaps weren't there as often.

We relied on our defender to make the tackle, although that didn't always work out. In general we had to tackle one player and that applied throughout the team. We would talk on the field and say: 'You tackle him, I'll get the next,' and that worked for us. We knew with more than one or two in the tackle we would be vulnerable around the ruck and flanks.

We realised we had good players and they could make the tackles when they were needed. The opposition were trying to do that too, but when the likes of Cliff Watson ran in with three or four people trying to tackle him, we were unstoppable. Teams couldn't one man tackle that guy at all, and that was good for the likes of me who fed off his offloads or the next play the ball afterwards.

Was it dangerous to leave someone else to tackle? It wasn't really, as we believed that they were all good players. These days there are sometimes four or five men in a tackle and I know that the extra man in is used to hurt the player with the ball sometimes. But I think a multi-man tackling team gives an advantage to the opposition because of the gaps created. I revert back to Watson and what he used to do. The ploy really was to get a quick play the ball to exploit those gaps. That's what we wanted. If we used these gaps, then the opposition would hold down and it would be a penalty. In my day, I could kick and score two points, then have another six tackles. Rugby can be such a simple game!

I think another problem is everyone knows each team's set moves. There isn't much variety in the modern game. You get the odd run around, and players running lines, but never as much as in my day. It was a breath of fresh air recently when the Saints played and Sean Long spotted a gap and sent the ball over three players for the winger to go in. That showed the vision that can be lacking a little bit in the Super League. The gap was created when Saints' opposition four-man tackled someone, the player played the ball quickly, Sean missed someone out and it was a walk in. It was good to watch and I wish there was more of it in the modern game.

The five drives and kick, or the move of passing behind two players is used too much. There's little variety and that means we struggle against Australia who successfully try these tactics. It would also be also be nice to see players run the ball on the last tackle too. These days the wingers drop back on the last expecting the kick return but that means, in the right circumstances, you can exploit the space they leave. If you get it wide then there is some extra space if you get it to your winger. Then they can decide whether to come inside, or chip over, that sort of thing. The winger has 20 or 30 yards before he needs to make a decision. The important thing is to have control of the ball. When you kick it you don't have the same control. Of course these are risky plays, but they do work.

That said, the modern game can be a delight to watch. The big games, the finals, are tense, but that's when the best players come to the fore. The likes of Sean Long, Keiron Cunningham, Kevin Sinfield and Paul Sculthorpe always shine in these games and do something spectacular. They were brought up with the game and it shows in their passion for it, and in their desire to appear on the big stage.

I know a lot of people think the game is quicker than it was, but I don't think there is much difference to when we had the four tackle rule in the late seventies and early eighties. With just four tackles for teams to do their stuff in, they would kick on the third or fourth tackle, and that seemed a little panicky to me. It was almost like seven's rugby. It quickened the game up of course, but we ended up kicking for kicking's sake, much like in rugby union.

Some union teams don't even follow their kick and league ended up like that in the four tackle rule too. We didn't want to get caught with the ball so we booted it into the opposition's area and hopefully made them turn around and do something with it. Or we hoped to get it back in the scrum as we could in those days. Scrummaging was proper scrummaging in those days too; hookers hooked and fought for the ball.

So is the modern game faster? The four tackle rule existed in the olden days and I certainly don't think the modern game is as fast as it was in those days. It is touch and go though. But if you look at the days of the unlimited tackle, teams could keep the ball all day so the modern game has to be quicker than that. That's not to say the invention wasn't there in the unlimited days—teams had a choice. You could bring people in and flip it out into the wings and exploit the gaps. Or you could keep it all day!

In any case, in my era and this one, players were fit and could keep going all day. Substitutions only came in the sixties and we used them sparingly and really only for injuries. The game now uses subs very well, and there are players that are specifically designed, I think, for that impact role. In general with modern day training and nutrition, players are fitter. And so they should be with the amount of time they spend in the gym. It is their place of work after all, so they should be able to spend more time getting 'game ready'. Whether they would be fitter than the coal miner, the brewery worker or Tommy Bishop lifting 56-pound sacks of potatoes, I don't know. Doing that all day would get you fit.

There were fit players in my days too; they just did different things for their 'normal' day jobs. Of course, the sprints are faster these days meaning the game is a little quicker and players are more 'tuned' into match day. I don't think it would affect the 'has been' player as they would be fit with physical work. Personally, I enjoyed being a drayman. I jumped up and down on a wagon all day, lifting barrels and that kept me going. I had a variety of things to do to my body whether that was lifting or running and I had the odd beer too, which kept me going. I never really liked to lift heavy weights, preferring to lift dumbbells to keep me in trim. I have seen players who were quick runners lose that speed because they were doing too many weights.

What's good for one person, isn't good for another, but I just liked using dumbbells. For the modern player, as it was back then, upper body strength is important and I know that training comes in at a young age now. They have all the right nourishment and they get pampered! It's come a long way since Stan McCormack's days! I think it is an important time in a player's development and they should be happy to be looked after. They get told when to drink, eat and they get the right supplements and have massages. They should enjoy it whilst they can because if they are injured, the game spits them out quickly.

I have never understood the fascination with wrestling. I think it affects how players tackle. A lot of players lift the leg of the tackled player these days and that isn't a tackle. That's just going in to hurt the person and isn't right. Wrestling brought that into the game a little more. In my view James Roby tackles correctly.

He goes with the player and uses the correct technique. You can't see the wrestling in his game. Wrestling and rugby league don't go together.

The kick to the corner on the last tackle crept into the game in the late seventies and I'll be buggered why we didn't think of it earlier. The Aussies brought it into the game and it is a heavily used play these days. Kicking to the corner, or an up and under on the last tackle is a 50:50 play. Two people go up and one catches the ball fair and square. When the winger scores off that kick—is it because they are good at handling the ball, or is it because a defender isn't good at defending?

It's a good ploy, even if it's a little repetitive and I don't know why we didn't do that in the sixties. Looking back, we had wingers who could catch the ball with great athleticism. But as I say, teams do rely on it a little too much. Close to the line there is rarely anything else these days. There aren't any real moves, teams either pass the ball behind the player or chip through. There isn't a lot variation compared to the variation in the 'olden' days.

At the end of the day though, from the tackle a player can only go forward, left or right! The ploy of the acting half back scooting from dummy half is dangerous especially with the likes of Keiron Cunningham and James Roby in a team. Perhaps the markers should stop this play a little more. If they stood a yard away from the play the ball they could see what happens and make the right decision from there. Markers seem to want to get as tight as possible to the man playing the ball. If they stand a yard back and the play the ball man moves forward, they should be collared too.

In my view, referees allow the man playing the ball too much freedom. Watch any game these days and they will walk forward, sneak yards on their knees or not play the ball correctly: basically they get away with doing what they want. When they gain a yard or two that means the opposition are offside when the ball is played. That is what is wrong with the game; the play the ball is a mess. The player playing the ball obstructs so nobody can tackle the acting half back. That would have been interpreted as obstruction in my day. It needs cleaning up in my view.

I know I have mentioned that there is little variation on the last tackle. I think teams should try something different. Some teams kick on the first tackle and catch out the opposition. When Darren Albert was at Saints and Sean Long was younger they caught teams out with this play. I just wish players would bear in mind that there are spaces to exploit—especially on the last tackle when the wingers go back.

If we had 40:20s in my day, we would have murdered teams. I can't believe it isn't used much. You get the ball back so what's stopping you doing it on the first tackle? There are kickers available. Leeds have three or four, Saints have the same. There is space to exploit. Yet teams seem reluctant to do it. Of course, it has to be done at the right time. And if they do, they save all that energy of getting 50 yards up the field through five tackles! Teams should back themselves more.

The moves come from the training pitch and from coaches, but a player on the field needs to call it. Players don't invent the moves in a match; they need someone to exploit it in the game. There is a lack of fresh moves to unlock tight defences. The variation of these stops players rushing up and having to do it all themselves. If you kick on the first or second tackle then the winger might go back in readiness because they haven't a clue what you might do. It places doubt in the opposition's mind and that is what all good rugby league players want to do.

I know I have been harping on about penalties but I also believe the drop goal is a dying art too. It can be used to make the opposition think about what is happening and they worry about suddenly having to score twice or whatever. In one game I watched Saints drop a goal with 10 minutes to go then with two minutes left, we were losing by a point. We were in front of their sticks and were set up, but decided to go for the try instead. Why did we do this? Players will always back themselves to score of course but where is the sense in this? We could have got the ball back and perhaps had chance to drop another! At least we would have been assured of not losing.

Kicking drop goals is a dying art in terms of putting extra pressure on the opposition. The example above is a perfect illustration of this. The drop goal was set up, but then the player—in this case Sean Long—saw a gap and went wide. However if the drop goal was set up and he thought there was a chance to score a try, then that is different. In hindsight he made the wrong decision, but at least it showed he was thinking. And that isn't a bad thing. If he thought he would score a try then I can't be overly critical of him in that situation. I have a lot of time for Sean Long and I believe that he is a real thinker as well as a hard worker who tackles well. He is a great player who does things on instinct at the spur of the moment. He will take opportunities and he is the one person who can do it. He goes outside and takes the ball in. Although he can be criticised for doing things wrong, his overall play shows what a good player he is. He isn't just on the glory trail. He will throw a long ball and knows what to do at the right time. In this case he chose the wrong option. He was in position and should have popped it over, but at least he thought 'outside the box' and went for it. I know I have contradicted myself here, but I hope you know what I mean!

Perhaps players think a point isn't good enough. But, a drop goal used right can mean a point for a draw or can push a team in front. It is mind over matter. It was the same in the 2008

Grand Final when Saints were eight points behind. They got a penalty in front of the sticks and decided to go for the try. With two scores ahead, a team feels more confident. With a penalty conversion, Leeds would have lost some of their confidence. These kind of opportunities need to be taken in my view. If Long had kicked the goal it would have been game on. Sometimes you have to play the percentages. You have the ball so kick the goal and maintain the momentum. A drop goal makes the opposition nervous. Making the opposition score twice to win isn't a big thing. Think about it: if you are six points up, a drop goal will make it seven points and the opposition have to score twice. This is an important tactic.

The likes of Sean, Scully and Andy Farrell were big parts of the international game and even though we have players coming through, we don't seem to have hit some of the highs of when they played. We are always capable of beating Australia in one off games, but stringing a series together seems to be difficult. And for some reason, we are now losing to New Zealand as well.

Modern fans still have the passion for international rugby league. At the last few World Club Challenges there have been 30,000 plus inside the stadiums and that shows good support for what is basically a club match. But we just hope the same fans will turn up at the end of the season for an Ashes, Test Series or Tri-Nations. The passion is there and the authorities need to harness that swell of national pride at those events. Waiting 10 months for the next event to come around isn't the way to go.

With regards to the team selection process, I'm not sure it is right for the international game. You can't really argue with the majority of the last England team in the 2008 World Cup being from Saints and Leeds but it shouldn't have taken Tony Smith so long to announce that team. That's not his fault though—he wanted to see all the players in action before deciding, but it meant he drew out the build up to the tournament.

Perhaps the way to go is to have a selection committee. Like the 'Big Five' of the old Welsh rugby union with, say, five independent people sat on it. I know I have criticised the selection policy of some committees who are made up of chairmen who promote their own players. It might be the right time for an independent committee to pick the best 20 or so players available rather than the coach. You could take on board the coach's opinion, but in the end a band of people much like the ECB in cricket would select the team. They wouldn't pick by reputation or on who has been a good player in the past, but on who could do a job and who is playing well at that time. The coach could then prepare the team, watch them train and get the selection right.

I maintain the coach should have a say as he can watch some of the players throughout the year, but mainly the committee should select his players. The committee would be expected to watch as many games as they could and see how certain partnerships work on the field. But they would hand over the team to the coaching staff and not get involved in the day to day running of the team. In this way, they would pick the players in top form and decide which player can do a job at which position because they are on fire. They need to be playing well before selection and the coach has to finalise the team.

In the past we have had a good base of players, but we have sometimes only picked players because they were already on the team. I stress again that we have to pick players who are playing the best at the time and then have the bottle to let them go if they aren't ready. Players have to be selected on merit and not just because Collins plays the piano or because he usually gives another player a lift. It has actually happened that a player has been chosen because he provides a lift for someone else. Collins deserved his 10 caps by the way!

Splitting up the Great Britain team was good for a few players outside the England team who wouldn't have made the GB squad. It gave them a chance of being an international instead of waiting for a GB call up. It was great for me back in the sixties and seventies to play for Wales and it is great for Scots, Welsh and Irish players too as they can play for their national team instead of being left out in the cold. I do believe that the GB Lions should have been retained though as that added an extra incentive for players to work hard.

You need a full team of Scots, Irish and Welsh players rather than just a few. You can't bend the rules so you have a few Scot players, for example, and then a load of overseas players. It's great, providing you stick to the grandparent rule. Teams like Wales will get 40 points put on them, but they need the game time or how will they ever progress? It's simple to me really.

That is why what is currently happening in South Wales excites me. At the Crusaders, I can see what they are trying to do and I pray it will be successful. I think that the side, in a few years time, needs to be predominately Welsh. At the moment there are a lot of overseas players in there but I think eventually you need the majority of players to be from the club's country or local area. Nothing against the 'foreigners'—they were needed initially to start off the team but the team needs a local angle to get the locals interested. That's difficult to achieve in a short time, but it has to happen to make the locals feel part of the club. The more Welsh players at Crusaders, the bigger the crowds will be and this will benefit the game of rugby league as a whole. There are many feeder clubs in the area, the players are there and you have to get them playing the game. Rugby league has so much potential down there to be big but to do this, unlocking the talent is paramount. I can only see a good future for it.

In the past players went down to Cardiff when they were over the hill and it detracted from the club and the game. Cardiff signed players who had gone through their benefits. They wanted to succeed but fans expected a little more. They wanted to see great players play like their reputations and careers suggested, but that was never going to happen. You have to start from within and flower, rather than go outside. They needed to get the youngsters playing. But it will take hard work, time, money and patience. Perseverance is key. Yes, the Crusaders have three years, but it will take a generation for these kids to come through. People throughout the game have to understand the team needs long-term support.

Finally, I'd like to think the modern day player could fit into my era and vice versa. Sean Long, Paul Sculthorpe, Keiron Cunningham and Kevin Sinfield could drop into any team in my era because they are good rugby players. James Roby would fit in our era because he is a textbook tackler and would have done well in our one man tackling system. He is virtually the only player in the league who tackles correctly. Cunningham was brought up hooking the ball and he would fit into the team. Chris Joynt was another player with excellent handling skills. They would all have done well.

So how many players from my era would fit into the modern game? How many do you want? Alex Murphy, Frank Myler, Cliff Watson...the list is endless. Look at my dream team. Any of those guys would rip it up. These players changed the rules and set up the game we watch today. That's how good they were. You can't say they wouldn't do well. Good players will always come out on top.

19

'BUGGER IT, I'M GOING TO ENJOY THE MOMENT...'

I have come full circle. I signed for St Helens Rugby League Club in 1962 and the buggers still haven't shaken me off. I have been at Saints as a player, assistant coach, head coach, marketing and sales manager, football manager and now gameday manager. It has been a heck of a journey and I regret nothing.

In 2008, I was named Honorary Life President and despite it being spelt incorrectly on the certificate I was given (good spot Jacqueline!) I am thoroughly delighted. It might be something and nothing, or maybe they chose me because no one came to mind, or they had no one else, but it's an honour all the same! I am not a local lad, yet Chairman Eamonn McManus and the Board of Directors still chose me. When I signed all those years ago, I didn't know where I was going or what was in front of me. I only came to play rugby league so to end up as Life President is unbelievable and puts the icing on the cake. As I have come through the ranks as a player and coach, this is a real honour and makes it all worthwhile.

It was a privilege to play and be part of the club before I was given this role, but to be still involved with Saints after all this time just tops it off. One thing though—I still have to buy my own beer at Knowsley Road!

As I got older I realised how much my family meant to me. That sounds like I forgot them all those years earlier, but I refer to my family as the club and my wonderful wife, three daughters and seven grandchildren. They are in my heart and always will be. I loved going home after training, working and playing to see them. I am very proud of them for their support and it was a great feeling to know they were behind me all the time. I have always had them following me with confidence as I matured and grew up and I am eternally grateful. If it hadn't been for them then I just don't know where I would have ended up. I couldn't have asked for a better family. They are perfect. When I had ups and downs through injury and other things they were great. So, Jacqueline and all of you, I love you and I am very proud of you. You have always been there and I want to thank you from the bottom of my heart.

I know I am coming to the end of my story, but throughout the process of writing this book, I have been thinking about how I would like to be remembered. And the short answer is I don't know! I don't think I have meant anyone any harm. I have had to disappoint and tell off players and people and I never meant any of them any harm. I just said the things I needed to say at the time and moved on. I suppose it's up to you as to how you remember me. I have no regrets at all. You can say things didn't work out, there were good days and bad days, but I wouldn't want to swap with anyone. This hand I have had has been brilliant. I am happy with it and count myself lucky. It has been fantastic all the way and I have loved every minute.

Writing a book is a strange experience. It is a great and uplifting process to think and talk about your life. Sometimes you don't want to say too much yet on other subjects you just fly! I have brought up things I had forgotten about. I have seen forgotten faces and friends in my head. I have reminisced on good and bad times and it has been a great experience for me. That's why I have enjoyed it.

I hadn't given any thought about doing something like this before. But now it is over I am excited and delighted. I have done it for my family so they can see my whole career laid out in front of them. They have had a lot to put up with! I have been away for long periods of time working, training, playing, on tour and such and at times they wouldn't have seen me for days. I'm sure the kids forgot about me too! So, this book shows what I have been up to and proves I wasn't on the skive! This is what all those hours away were about. I was doing all this! I did it all for you and hopefully you will understand why I missed school concerts and things like that.

I dedicate this book simply to my wife, kids and grandkids. I love you all.

Not bad for a village boy.

KEL COSLETT TRIBUTES

Mel James (St Helens, 1972–83)
I had not met Kel until I signed for Saints in 1972 and he made me very welcome in the team. Kel always controlled the games and it worked very well, as the records show!

Ron Hoofe (Saints commentator)
He was among the best, if not the greatest Welshman to don a Saints' jersey. He was a gentleman, a great clubman and a versatile player who possessed a great rugby brain and what a tackling machine he was! He still looks fit enough to play!

Dave Thomas (Aberavon)
One of my first memories of Kel is playing against him when he was at Llanelli. I was playing for Aberavon at the time and I made a break and he came across and absolutely whacked me, sending me flying. I had a full season under my belt and felt I was a hardened player but he hit me hard—much harder than his 17 years showed.

When he joined Aberavon he turned up in the dressing room dressed like a teddy boy. He wore a long navy coat, blue crepe suit, heels that were at least an inch-and-a-half high and yellow socks!

He was a great kicker of the ball though and that kick at Swansea was easily his best goal. The conditions were terrible, muddy, wet and the leather ball was sodden through. Rory O'Connor our captain, told him to have a crack at a 50-yard penalty attempt from the touchline, which if it went over would secure the game. The Swansea fans were giving him some real stick as he took it, but he gave it a hell of a boot and it went over. As he ran back Kelvin said: 'That'll bloody shut them up!'

Billy Benyon (St Helens, 1962–77)
Kel was a great colleague and teammate, a real genuine clubman and a great professional.

Keith Northey (St Helens, 1961–65)
As a player he was phenomenal. He played everywhere from fullback, loose forward and prop. It was always very reassuring to know you had him at the back, and his goal kicking was tremendous. He was a great player and top as a man too. Kel was actually a very quiet man—well he used to be—not like now when you get him out with a few beers! He would never do something like when Jack Arkwright accidentally used Wintergreen on his backside and balls instead of Vaseline!

Cyril Jones (Aberavon)
That kick against Swansea is still spoken about in this area to this day. He kicked the penalty on the 50-yard line and the fans were laughing at him. He kicked it; it didn't leave more than two yards off the floor and kept rising—going over the crossbar. It was a long kick in those days with a leather ball too. The Swansea crowd were giving him a bit of jip beforehand.

John Warlow (St Helens, 1963–69, 73–75)
We first met when I came out of the army after completing my National Service. I went down to Llanelli to take part in the probables versus possibles game and Kel was on the possibles

side. I came off with a cut head at half time and we all got changed in the same dressing room. After, he asked me to go for a pint and we have been friends ever since. We met after every Aberavon or Llanelli (because that's who I played for) home game half way for a night out. And when I headed north I'm sure he put in a good word, although he has never admitted it to me.

I remember he came down to pick me up and take me to St Helens and he took me to his digs for a meal. It was a great welcome and the rest of the boys turned up and we went out for a few drinks. That's Kel—he's that sort of person. He is a real genuine fella, who would do you a good turn. We were best mates and he was the best man at my wedding.

I still remember when he broke his nose at Featherstone. I sat next to him at half time in the dressing room and he asked me how bad it looked. I said it was all right, good, as long as he didn't look in the mirror.

Playing wise, he's done it all.

Peter Harvey (St Helens 1963–66)

Put simply, Kel Coslett is himself. He calls himself 'a boy from the valleys' and that is his perennial put down. St Helens expected their rugby union signings to be the best around and Kel was the best goal kicking fullback in Wales at the time. When he came up here, he continued in that vein. He then became a forward of note after he broke his leg.

He was a remarkable fullback, dependable, very good at tackling, a great colleague and like all Welshman, he couldn't sing! Williams, Mantle, Coslett, they were all good companions indeed. He is very loyal and worked very hard. He was just as at home in the St Helens team as I was as a local boy. From where I was, Kel seemed at home from very early days. By his very nature, he mixed well with the people of St Helens and seemed to become part of the local scene very quickly.

John Collins (Aberavon)

Like most of the people down in Aberavon and Swansea, we remember the day Kel kicked that conversion off the touchline. Before that, we had been picked to play in Cornwall and had had a few beers the night before. So when we came to get our train at 9 a.m. in the morning, we were in a real hurry. When we got to Bristol we had to change trains, ended up on the wrong platform and train and set off back to Plymouth.

By the time we got to the game a couple of lads were getting changed so they had a vote to see whether we could play. We did play and Kelvin won the game with that fabulous kick, with the old fashioned ball in the wind and rain, from just over half way. He was very popular with the players and the fans. I played the piano and he sang well. He is a very good singer.

Wilf Smith (St Helens and Wigan)

I was one of the first to meet him when he joined Saints and was the first to show him how to play the ball. I think I had hurt my shoulder and the coach asked me to show him how to play the ball for half an hour. I was his number two at Wigan. I was plastering at the time and he asked me to come and join him. Wigan were in dire straits when he went over as they had only won one game. I went there when they had about 12 games to go and out of the 17 games Kel coached, he won 12. He sorted out the discipline issues and really made Wigan a decent team. I think if he had stayed at Wigan, his coaching career would have been longer. I think if he had done another year, he would have been there at least another five.

I admire Kel. He had a lot of bad luck when he joined Saints, when he broke his ankle, but he worked hard. You hear a lot of people saying that he should have done this or that, but Kel just did it.

John Walsh (St Helens 1968–75)

I have three strong memories of Kel. Firstly, in the 1960s and 1970s high tackling was more or less the norm and two-man tackling was quite common. Kel was a bugger for coming in as the second tackler after you had stood up and I got more smacks in the mouth from Kel than from any opposing players.

Secondly, in my playing days we won every trophy that was available and Kel was captain for many of them. Needless to say a few drinks were consumed after the victories. At the end of the evening Kel would put his arms round your shoulder, give you a big grin and say something profound. I assume it was something profound, as due to the combination of drink and his Welsh accent, which got stronger after a few drinks, I had no idea what he actually said. I found that smiling and agreeing with him worked wonders. In 2002, when we had a reunion for the 1972 Wembley victory, he did exactly the same thing. I guess old habits die hard.

Finally, we were playing a home game and we had a Welsh trialist listed as A.N. Other. In the programme, he was described as six foot tall and weighing 16 stone. As we were stripping for the game, Frankie Barrow turned to Kel and the other Welsh players and in a dead serious manner asked them if there were only 10 inches in a Welsh foot. After an intro like that the trialist didn't play well and was never heard of again.

Geoff Pimblett (St Helens 1970–79)

I signed in 1970 and we have been friends ever since. Kel is a person you can rely on and who will give you an honest view on a situation. He would not knowingly let anybody down and he's very good at assessing a situation and doing the right thing. On the field you were always guaranteed two points from goal kicks, even if it did take two minutes for him to string the ball. Naturally, his goal kicking was a real bonus, but he was also the pivot for most of the team's play—especially in organisation.

He would always come up with something others couldn't do. With Saints on tour in 1976, I remember we played Auckland in a sea of mud. You couldn't pick your feet out of it. I was kicking goals, without tees in those days, and I just couldn't lift the ball at all. Kel took over, and from the touchline toe ended a beauty over the posts! He left those boots in New Zealand—it was his last game for the Saints.

We had many beers together and have been members of the Sprayhurst Club in St Helens since 1972 after his dad took us there. As a team we would socialise a lot and Wembley trips bonded the players and their wives. Friendships were struck and as the years panned out our two families went on holiday together and that has continued until the present day. We have shared some good times and helped each other through difficult ones too. With all the honours he's received at Saints over his 45 years or so, we'll never get him back to Wales. Kel—I'm glad I've had you as a mate for all these years!

Daniel Anderson (St Helens 2005–08)

Personally, I would like to thank Kel Coslett for his support in my time at Saints. Kel, from my first day in the job, was very accessible and helpful. He is a humorous man, always finding time for a great yarn about his rugby league adventure that was 531 games for Saints. My favourite was the pie and milk midnight feast after a night on the turps. Kel is a knowledgeable rugby man. His quiet summation of our status during a game was never far from fact and could spot technical flaws in our goal kickers whilst studying the form for a Haydock twilight meeting. It is my pleasure to have spent three-and-a-half years with this genuine fella.

Ken Thomas (Aberavon)

When Kel told me about his offer from Saints and the fee they were offering, I told him to sign straightaway! Within a fortnight he had signed. So, it's my fault that Aberavon lost a good player. He never regretted going north and he always makes the trip home for club dinners.

We were out in Tenerife one summer and this kid came in with the St Helens' jersey on with Newlove on the back. I didn't say anything, then the little boy was running round and I asked him whether he liked Newlove. I told him I had a friend who used to play for Saints. His mother heard and I told her it was Kel Coslett. She went missing for around quarter of an hour and when she came back she had been talking to her mother about someone who knew Kel really well. That's what his name means to people.

I know a lot of people will have mentioned that goal at Swansea, but it was a special moment. They were late coming home, but we argued to let Kel play. It was raining, we were losing, and right from the half line and the touchline he knocked it over.

Roy Mathias (St Helens 1972–83)

I know all his weaknesses! He is a genuine bloke and a real character. On the field he controlled everything and it all revolved around Kel. I came from the same town and he came down to talk me into signing for Saints! Leigh came in for me as did Warrington and I didn't know what to do. I asked 'Is it all right?' and he said it was. I asked him if it was hard and he said it was, so I got no sense out of him at all. Rugby union was a different game to rugby league and it was hard, but both he and Geoff helped me out.

He seemed only to wash his training kit, say, twice a year, and with him working on the wagons and such it was pretty bad! But he is a genuine bloke who was a real grafter and points scorer. The Welsh lads meet up now and again and it is still a riot. Kel offers his tips, but I say I have never had a winner from him either. I've heard people have the odd one, and he offers 'certs' now and again, but I have never had one. His last 'cert' is still running now.

Frank Myler (St Helens 1967–71)

Kel was a great player, a real team man. I always thought he was a little underestimated by some people. This first time ball they talk about in football, well it is the same in rugby league. You need to have a good pair of hands to get it going. I played as stand off and Kel was inside me. I looked outside and when I wanted the ball, he was the man.

He was one of those players who was always there in attack and defence. I think he should have had more international recognition. The fact he never went on tour amazes me, because he was certainly good enough. Off the field, all the players got on well together and we had a lot of good times. For him to stay 14 years at Saints tells you how good he was. He was involved in their glory periods and he had to be an exceptional player to last that long. He is an exceptional bloke.

Eamonn McManus (Chairman, St Helens)

If there was a person I would single out as the most consistently dedicated servant to Saints at every level of the last three or four generations, then it would surely be Kel Coslett.

As a boy I watched him toe poke those old leather balls over the posts from all over the field and grace the fullback and loose forward positions at Saints during a great decade in our history. For him to captain the 'Dad's Army' Saints to a memorable 1976 Challenge Cup victory over a favoured Widnes was my standout memory of his Saints career.

As a man and as a gentleman he has graced our club over the decades with his presence and has had a wonderful influence on players, staff and supporters alike. I have been blessed with many great memories and privileges during my tenure as the Chairman of the great St Helens Club. At the top of my list must go appointing Kel Coslett as our Life President in 2008. He typifies all that makes our club so respected throughout the world, and has been at the cause of many of the reasons for our success. He is a friend and a colleague and I look forward to many more years of enjoyable success with Kel at our side.

John Mantle (St Helens 1964–75)

As we both travelled the same path to St Helens, I know the difficulties we both had in adapting to a new and different game. We both met and married local girls and have long become St Heleners. We are both settled in St Helens.

I actually played my first and last game for Saints in the same team as Kel. My first game was against Wigan 'A' Team and Kel played after suffering a broken leg—it was his comeback game. I also played my last game in the Championship Final in 1976 with Kel as my fellow prop—this was a week after beating Widnes in the Challenge Cup Final at Wembley. We had been written off as having no chance against the younger Widnes props.

We had been christened 'Dads Pack' (Dad's Army)—too old to take on the young Widnes props. History will show that we played them off the park in a temperature of plus 100 and this was at only 34 years of age. The following week we repeated the performance by winning the Championship Final. These two performances rank as the highlight of my career at Saints and I am sure they are among Kel's favourite moments, especially as he was captain.

We were both fortunate to play in very good teams throughout our playing careers. Kel was a good captain for years and an astute tactician. He was a great teammate. He put me through many gaps with our various moves. His conversion from fullback to being a forward was one of the success stories at Saints.

Finally, I must comment on his goal-kicking—he was, without doubt, one of the best goal kickers I have seen in both codes of rugby. He rarely missed kicks at goal. When he did miss, it was usually by inches. His ability to kick so accurately was born out of good technique and continual practice. Kel was a perfectionist—he always spent time practising his kicking—even in the latter years of his career.

It was an honour to know him and play in the same team as him. I also have had the privilege of playing in the Welsh RL team with him. I thought so much about him as a fellow player and as a person that I even named my son after him.

Tom Van Vollenhoven (1957–67)
I first met Kel Coslett in 1962 when he joined Saints from Wales where he was a rugby union international. Kel was, and still is, a very amiable and friendly person. I remember sitting in the dressing room before a match. In those days we used pieces of string to tie up our socks. Coming from union, Kel had his own elastic garters. As we sat in the dressing room we heard this Welsh accent shouting to Walter Jones our kit man: 'Walter, where's my garters?' The whole dressing room packed up laughing.

Kel became the League's top goal-kicker in 1962–63 but unfortunately, he broke his ankle in 1964 and didn't play for a long time. When he came back he moved to loose forward where he was just as outstanding as he was at fullback. In later years, after I retired, Kel became the Saints' captain. He served the club well over the years. He played the most games ever for Saints, more than 500, and stayed with the club after he retired. He's doing wonderful work in helping with the day-to-day running of the club.

I was over the moon when I got the news that Kel had been made Honorary Life President. Leonie and I wish Kel and Jackie all the best in the future. Well done Kel, my old mate!

Terry Davies (Llanelli and Wales)

I remember Kelvin coming to me when he was having a problem with his kicking at Aberavon. He was drifting the ball wide and missing a number of goals. We trained together a lot and one day I went down to the field with him and I was on the floor watching his kicking action. I could see he was all over the place so I asked him to do a little dance to get his balance and then when he felt comfortable he could strike the ball. That seemed to solve it and I remember Eddie Waring used to say on his commentary that everyone should watch Kelvin's dance!

We would kick for hours and sometimes we would kick the old leather ball round by the time we had finished. I also remember when he travelled with me and the Welsh team to France as a reserve. We were sharing a room and then my brother came over on the boat and had nowhere to stay. We smuggled him into our room, three to a bed, and he had to hide whenever they brought breakfast up to the room.

But if I had to sum up Kelvin it would be like this. I did my National Service and there were some tough people there with me. But the only person I would want alongside me in the trenches would be Kelvin. You could rely on him to do anything and he would always be alongside you. I cannot speak highly enough of him. He always has a wide grin on his face and says he owes me everything. But he did it all himself and is a real ambassador for not only the village of Bynea but also for Wales too. He deserves every success and everything that is due to him. He is a true friend.

APPENDIX

Rugby league statistics

Team/Season	PLD	TRY	GLS	PTS
St Helens				
1962–63	44	3	156	321
1963–64	41	5	138	291
1964–65	9	2	26	58
1965–66	26+2	4	57	126
1966–67	15+3	1	3	9
1967–68	38+1	4	84	180
1968–69	46+1	3	154	317
1969–70	42	1	160	323
1970–71	49	3	193	395
1971–72	54	8	214	452
1972–73	46	2	162	330
1973–74	39+2	4	134	280
1974–75	39	2	120	246
1975–76	31+2	3	38	85
Totals	**519+11**	**45**	**1639**	**3413**

Team/Season	PLD	TRY	GLS	DRP	PTS
Rochdale					
1976–77	17+1	1	0	0	3
1977–78	13+1	0	23	0	46
1978–79	17	2	15	1	37
Totals	**47+2**	**3**	**38**	**1**	**86**

Total club career

Team/Season	PLD	TRY	GLS	DRP	PTS
St Helens	519+11	45	1639	0	3413
Rochdale	47+2	3	38	1	86
Totals	**566+13**	**48**	**1677**	**1**	**3499**

Representative

Team/Season	PLD	TRY	GLS	DRP	PTS
Wales**	13	1	8	0	19
Wales 1975 tour*	4	1	10	0	23
Other Nationalities	1	0	2	0	4
Totals	**18**	**2**	**20**	**0**	**46**

* To Australia and New Zealand. Not including World Cup matches.

** Includes one non-full international.

Grand totals

Team/Season	PLD	SUB	TRY	GLS	DRP	PTS
St Helens	519	12	45	1,639	0	3,413
Rochdale Hornets	47	2	3	38	1	86
Wales	13	0	1	8	0	19
Wales 1975 tour	4	0	1	10	0	23
Other Nationalities	1	0	0	2	0	4
Grand totals	**584**	**14**	**50**	**1,697**	**1**	**3,545**

Thanks to Ray Fletcher, Bill Bates, Alex Service and the Saints Historical Society for their help in compiling these stats. Please note: Kel's drop goal stats for St Helens are incomplete. Drops were worth the same as goals and therefore, deciphering the two is impossible.

Coaching records

Rochdale Hornets
November 1976 to August 1979

Wigan
October 1979 to April 1980

St Helens
June 1980 to May 1982

Coaching record

1976–77 First Division

Pos	Team	PLD	W	D	L	FR	AG	PT
1	Featherstone Rovers	30	21	2	7	568	334	44
2	St Helens	30	19	1	10	547	345	39
3	Castleford	30	19	1	10	519	350	39
4	Hull Kingston Rovers	30	18	1	11	496	415	37
5	Warrington	30	18	0	12	532	406	36
6	Salford	29*	17	1	11	560	402	35
7	Wigan	30	15	2	13	463	416	32
8	Bradford Northern	30	15	2	13	488	470	32
9	Leeds	29*	14	2	13	467	439	30
10	Widnes	30	15	0	15	403	393	30
11	Wakefield Trinity	0	13	2	15	487	480	28
12	Workington Town	30	13	1	16	352	403	27
13	**Rochdale Hornets**	**30**	**11**	**0**	**19**	**367**	**449**	**22**
14	Leigh	30	8	1	21	314	634	17
15	Barrow	30	8	0	22	345	628	16
16	Oldham	30	7	0	23	322	666	14

* Match abandoned and void.

1977–78 Second Division

Pos	Team	PLD	W	D	L	FR	AG	PT
1	Leigh	26	21	0	5	538	231	42
2	Barrow	26	21	0	5	521	234	42
3	**Rochdale Hornets**	**26**	**21**	**0**	**5**	**437**	**200**	**42**
4	Huddersfield	26	18	0	8	502	324	36
5	York	26	16	2	8	447	286	34
6	Oldham	26	17	0	9	419	325	34
7	Keighley	26	11	3	12	357	337	25
8	Swinton	26	11	1	14	369	385	23
9	Whitehaven	26	10	2	14	277	326	22
10	Huyton	26	9	2	15	250	352	20
11	Doncaster	26	9	0	17	304	528	18
12	Batley	26	5	1	20	233	496	11
13	Blackpool Borough	26	5	1	20	262	543	11
14	Halifax	26	2	0	24	182	531	4

1978–79 First Division

Pos	Team	PLD	W	D	L	FR	AG	PT
1	Hull Kingston Rovers	30	23	0	7	616	344	46
2	Warrington	30	22	0	8	521	340	44
3	Widnes	30	21	2	7	480	322	44
4	Leeds	30	19	1	10	555	370	39
5	St Helens	30	16	2	12	485	379	34
6	Wigan	30	16	1	13	484	411	33
7	Castleford	30	16	1	13	498	469	33
8	Bradford Northern	30	16	0	14	523	416	32
9	Workington Town	30	13	3	14	378	345	29
10	Wakefield Trinity	30	13	1	16	382	456	27
11	Leigh	30	13	1	16	406	535	27
12	Salford	30	11	2	17	389	435	24
13	Barrow	30	9	2	19	368	536	20
14	Featherstone Rovers	30	8	1	21	501	549	17
15	**Rochdale Hornets**	**30**	**8**	**0**	**22**	**297**	**565**	**16**
16	Huddersfield	30	7	1	22	314	725	15

1979–80 First Division

Pos	Team	PLD	W	D	L	FR	AG	PT
1	Bradford Northern	30	23	0	7	448	272	46
2	Widnes	30	22	1	7	546	293	45
3	Hull	30	18	3	9	454	326	39
4	Salford	30	19	1	10	495	374	39
5	Leeds	30	19	0	11	590	390	38
6	Leigh	30	16	1	13	451	354	33
7	Hull Kingston Rovers	30	16	1	13	539	445	33
8	St Helens	30	15	2	13	505	410	32
9	Warrington	30	15	2	13	362	357	32
10	Wakefield Trinity	30	14	2	14	435	466	30
11	Castleford	30	13	2	15	466	475	28
12	Workington Town	30	12	2	16	348	483	26
13	**Wigan**	**30**	**9**	**3**	**18**	**366**	**523**	**21**
14	Hunslet	30	7	1	22	346	528	15
15	York	30	6	1	23	375	647	13
16	Blackpool Borough	30	5	0	25	230	613	10

1980–81 Slalom Lager Championship

Pos	Team	PLD	W	D	L	FR	AG	PT
1	Bradford Northern	30	20	1	9	447	345	41
2	Warrington	30	19	1	10	459	330	39
3	Hull Kingston Rovers	30	18	2	10	509	408	38
4	Wakefield Trinity	30	18	2	10	544	454	38
5	Castleford	30	18	2	10	526	459	38
6	Widnes	30	16	2	12	428	356	34
7	Hull	30	17	0	13	442	450	34
8	**St Helens**	**30**	**15**	**1**	**14**	**465**	**370**	**31**
9	Leigh	30	14	1	15	416	414	29
10	Leeds	30	14	0	16	388	468	28
11	Barrow	30	13	0	17	405	498	26
12	Featherstone Rovers	30	12	0	18	385	450	22
14	Salford	30	10	1	19	473	583	21
15	Workington Town	30	9	3	18	335	457	21
16	Oldham	30	7	2	21	362	563	16

1981–82 Slalom Lager Championship

Pos	Team	PLD	W	D	L	FR	AG	PT
1	Leigh	30	24	1	5	572	343	49
2	Hull	30	23	1	6	611	273	47
3	Widnes	30	23	1	6	551	317	47
4	Hull Kingston Rovers	30	22	1	7	565	319	45
5	Bradford Northern	30	20	1	9	425	332	41
6	Leeds	30	17	1	12	514	418	35
7	**St Helens**	**30**	**17**	**1**	**12**	**465**	**415**	**35**
8	Warrington	30	14	2	14	403	468	30
9	Barrow	30	13	0	17	408	445	26
10	Featherstone Rovers	30	12	1	17	482	493	25
11	Wigan	30	12	0	18	424	435	24
12	Castleford	30	10	1	19	486	505	21
13	Fulham	30	9	1	20	365	539	19
14	Wakefield Trinity	30	9	1	20	341	526	19
15	York	30	4	2	24	330	773	10
16	Whitehaven	30	2	3	25	224	565	7

Coaching career totals—league

PLD	W	D	L	FR	AG	PT
176	81	5	90	2397	2522	167

Club records and individual honours at St Helens

Most points in a career
Kel Coslett 3413

Most appearances in a career
531(12) Kel Coslett

**Most goals in a career
(including drop goals)**
1639 Kel Coslett

Most goals in a season
214 Kel Coslett 1971–72
193 Kel Coslett 1970–71

Most points in a season
452 Kel Coslett 1971–72

Played in every game in a season
1962–63

Lance Todd Winner
1972

Major domestic honours:

Rugby union:
Aberavon Wizards: Welsh Championship 1960–61

Rugby league:
St Helens: BBC2 Floodlit Trophy 1971–72, 1975–76
St Helens: Challenge Cup 1965–66†, 1971–72, 1975–76
St Helens: League Champions 1965–66*†, 1969–70*, 1970–71*
St Helens: First Division Champions 1974–75
St Helens: Leader's Shield 1964–65, 1965–66
St Helens: Lancs Cup 1962–63, 1963–64, 1967–68, 1968–69
St Helens: Premiership Trophy 1975–76
St Helens: Western Div Championship Final 1964
St Helens: Lancashire League: 1964–65, 1965–66, 1966–67, 1968–69

*1965–6, 1969–70 and 1970–71 was decided on a Top 16 Play off system.
† Kel did not play in the 1965–66 Challenge Cup or Championship final, but qualified for a medal on number of games played.

Rochdale: Promotion to Division One 1977–78

Rugby league finals involving Kel

Date	Opponents	Comp	Season	Venue	Score
May 22, 1976	Salford	Premiership Trophy	1975–76	N	15–2
May 8, 1976	Widnes	Challenge Cup	1975–76	N	20–5
Dec 16, 1975	Dewsbury	BBC2 Floodlit Trophy	1975–76	H	22–2
May 17, 1975	Leeds	Premiership Trophy	1974–75	N	11–26
May 18, 1974	Warrington	Merit Club Championship Trophy	1973–74	N	12–13
May 20, 1972	Leeds	Championship Trophy	1971–72	N	5–9
May 13, 1972	Leeds	Challenge Cup	1971–72	N	16–13
Dec 14, 1971	Rochdale	BBC2 Floodlit Trophy	1971–72	H	8–2
May 22, 1971	Wigan	Championship Trophy	1970–71	N	16–12
Dec 15, 1970	Leeds	BBC2 Floodlit Trophy	1970–71	A	5–9
Nov 28, 1970	Leigh	Lancs Cup	1970–71	N	4–7
May 16, 1970	Leeds	Championship Trophy	1969–70	N	24–12
Dec 17, 1968	Wigan	BBC2 Floodlit Trophy	1968–69	A	4–7
Oct 25, 1968	Oldham	Lancs Cup	1968–69	N	30–2
Dec 2, 1967	Warrington	Lancs Cup (Rep)	1967–68	N	13–10
Oct 7, 1967	Warrington	Lancs Cup	1967–68	N	2–2
May 22, 1965	Halifax	Championship Trophy	1964–65	N	7–15
May 16, 1964	Swinton	Western Div Champ	1963–64	N	10–7
Oct 26, 1963	Leigh	Lancs Cup	1963–64	N	15–4
Oct 27, 1962	Swinton	Lancs Cup	1962–63	N	7–4

Thanks to the Saints Historical Society for this information.

St Helens players who played with Kel

Alan Ashton, Alan Beddow, Alan Briers, Alan Gwilliam, Alan Whittle, Albert Halsall, Alexander Murphy, Allan Bishop, A.N. Other x 9, Anthony Atherton, Anthony Barrow, Anthony Karalius, Anthony Waller, Arthur Johnson, Austin Rhodes, Berwyn Jones, Brian Coward, Brian Glover, Brian Hogan, Brian Rowley, Bryan Todd, Cennyd Williams, Chris Wellman, Christopher Charles, Cliff Watson, D. Critchley, David Brown, David Campbell, David Eckersley, David Hull, David Markey,

David Taylor, David Wood, Dennis Lyon, Dennis Marsh, Derek Brown, Derek Noonan, Don Stilwell, Douglas Laughton, Douglas Warlow, Eddie Cunningham, Eric Chisnall, Eric Hughes, Eric Prescott, Eric Woodyer, Errol Van Niekirk, F. Hill, Frank Barrow, Frank Myler, Frank Taylor, Frank Ward, Frank Wilson, Frederick Leyland, G. Walker, Garth Robertson, Geoffrey Pimblett, George Case, George Nicholls, Gerald Morris, Gordon Edgerton, Graham Liptrot, Graham Rees, Harold Pinner, Ian Jones, J. Heaton, J. White, Jack Pimblett, James Mustard, Jeff Hitchen, Jeffrey Heaton, John Arkwright, John Donovan, John Houghton, John Mantle, John McGinn, John Stephens, John Tembey, John Walsh, John Wills, Joseph Donegan, Joseph Egan, Joseph Robinson, Karel 'Tom' Van Vollenhoven, Keiron Pickavance, Keith Ashcroft, Keith Northey, Kelvin Earl, Kenneth Gwilliam, Kenneth Halliwell, Kenneth Kelly, Kenneth Large, Kenneth Thompson, Kevin Kelly, Lance Davies, Len Ball, Len Killeen, Les Mara, Leslie Greenall, Leslie Jones, M. Marsden, Melvyn James, Mervyn Hicks, Michael Hope, Michael McNeil, Michael Mooney, Michael Murphy, Mick Sullivan, Mike Knowles, Neil Courtney, Paul Kelly, Peter Birchall, Peter Brown, Peter Douglas, Peter Gartland, Peter Glynn, Peter Goddard, Peter Harvey, Ray French, Ray Turner, Raymond Howard, Raymond Hughes, Richard Huddart, Robert Blackwood, Robert Burdell, Robert Dagnall, Robert Goulding, Robert Harper, Robert Prosser, Robert Wanbon, Roy Mathias, Stan Owen, Stephen Gobey, Steve Houghton, Terry Loughlin, Thomas Bishop, Thomas Cunningham, Thomas Pimblett, Wilfred Smith, William Barrow, William Benyon, William Hayes, William Lomax, William Major, William Platt, William Sayer, William Sheffield.

Rugby union stats

Stats are accurate in terms of points and games, but limited information is available on numbers of tries, conversions and penalties. Therefore, where applicable, the numbers of these are mentioned, but not included, in totals.

Team/Season	PLD	TRY	CON	DRP	PEN	PTS
Llanelli						
1959–60	10	-	-	-	-	63
1960–61	3	-	2	-	1	7
Totals	10	-	-	-	-	70

Team/Season	PLD	TRY	CON	DRP	PEN	PTS
Aberavon						
1960–61	33	-	43	-	34	188
1961–62	40	-	-	-	-	160
Totals	53	-	-	-	-	348

Total club career

Team/Season	PLD	TRY	CON	DRP	PEN	PTS
Llanelli	13	-	-	-	-	70
Aberavon	53	-	-	-	-	348
Totals	**66**	-	-	-	-	**418**

Representative

Team/Season	PLD	TRY	CON	DRP	PEN	PTS
Wales						
1961–62	3	0	0	0	1	3
Totals	**3**	**0**	**0**	**0**	**1**	**3**

* Five Nations was cut to four after the outbreak of Smallpox in Wales and foot-and-mouth in Ireland.

Grand totals

Team/Season	PLD	TRY	CON	DRP	PEN	PTS
Llanelli	13	-	-	-	-	70
Aberavon	53	-	-	-	-	348
Wales	3	-	-	-	-	3
Grand totals	**69**	-	-	-	-	**421**

Aberavon players who played with Kel in the Welsh Championship winning side of 1960–61

Alan Bamsey, Bryan Jones, Cliff Ashton, Cyril Jones, Dave Owen, Dave Thomas, Dennis Perry, Ieuan Prosser, Jim Evans, John Bamsey, John Collins, Ken Thomas, Len Cunningham, Owen Hughes, Peter Jones, Phil Morgan, Rhys Loveluck, Roger Michaelson, Rory O'Connor, Tony O'Connor.